Too Good To Be Forgotten

CHANGING AMERICA IN THE '60s AND '70s

DAVID OBST

John Wiley & Sons, Inc.
New York • Chichester • Weinheim • Brisbane • Singapore • Toronto

This publication is designed to provide accurate and authoritative information in regard to the subject matter covered. It is sold with the understanding that the publisher is not engaged in rendering professional services. If professional advice or other expert assistance is required, the services of a competent professional person should be sought.

Library of Congress Cataloging-in-Publication Data:

Obst, David.
    Too good to be forgotten : changing America in the '60s and '70s /
David Obst
        p.   cm.
    Includes index.
    ISBN 0-471-29538-8 (alk. paper)
    1. United States—Politics and government—1961–1963.   2. United
States—Politics and government—1963–1969.   3. United States—
Politics and government—1969–1974.   4. Vietnamese Conflict,
1961–1975.   5. Watergate Affair, 1972–1974.   6. United States—
Social conditions—1960–1980.   7. Obst, David.   8. Journalists—
United States—Biography.   I. Title.
E839.5.O28   1998
973.92—dc21   98-8720
                                                                          CIP

Printed in the United States of America

10 9 8 7 6 5 4 3 2 1

To Jane Gottlieb
My Dream Come True

CONTENTS

INTRODUCTION

A well-written life is almost as rare as a well-spent one . . .
THOMAS CARLYLE

Why read a book about David Obst and the events of the 60s and 70s? I guess, to paraphrase Sir Edmund Hillary, because I was there. I was at the Democratic convention in 1968 and at Berkeley in the late 60s. I helped break the My Lai massacre story that won the Pulitzer Prize. I assisted Daniel Ellsberg with the Pentagon papers, was the agent for Woodward and Bernstein's *All the President's Men* and John Dean's *Blind Ambition,* and played a role in changing journalism forever. In short, if something was happening in America during that tumultuous period, I was able—through chance, guile, and fortune—to be in the middle of it.

This is a book about being a baby boomer, about how the emergence of the youth culture, the Vietnam War, and Watergate left their imprint on our generation. It's a personal, anecdotal book in which, because I was lucky enough to have known many of the major players, I give the reader an inside look at the history of the period. The stories of these incidental heroes are fun and exciting. The results of their actions are still with us today.

This is also a book about baby boomers coming of age. It's the story of how we almost succeeded in stealing America from the grown-ups, were beaten back, and, by the inexorable process of

1

aging, became those very adults that we used to make such great fun of.

To later generations, the explosive 60s and 70s are known only through star-spangled sagas such as *Easy Rider, Hair, Coming Home, American Graffiti,* and *The Big Chill.* The real stories, though, are even better. Our generation tried to remedy the ills of the world with a radical call to freedom—free love, free drugs, free will. We reaped marijuana, renounced the Vietnam War, rebelled against the regime, roused a media revolution. I was part of the original cast for the Chicago riots, the student protests at Berkeley, the Black Panther rallies, and the numerous anti-war demonstrations in Washington. In short, I was there for the greatest show on earth.

The atomic bomb blazed my rite of passage to young adulthood. My generation's coming of age was paralleled by unprecedented change. We were the first to be raised with super console TVs, Ford Fairlanes, frozen foods, Hydrox cookies, Toni permanents, toy guns, Barbie dolls, ducktails, coonskin caps, Kelvinators, steady rings, worry beads, saddle shoes, Instamatics, and psyche-delics.

Having barely survived high school, I spent my early under-graduate years in Taiwan, trying to become a China scholar. I became fascinated with Chinese affairs and, when I finally had one, I was unceremoniously tossed out of the country. When I returned to America in 1968, my A-1 draft card dictated an imme-diate return to Asia, only this time the government wanted to send me to Vietnam to fight a war I didn't believe in. My fear of vio-lence, my respect for Asian civilization, and my refusal to kill my previous hosts elicited a prompt meeting with the draft board. The elders avoided my eyes, refused to shake my hand, but grudgingly released me to another war zone—graduate school. Berkeley in the fall of 1968 was a replay of my summer. In August I had been to the Chicago Democratic convention/riots, where my political consciousness was raised by Abbie Hoffman and his Yippie Party and the brutality of the Chicago police who had decided to teach us kids a lesson. Graduate school was likewise an education in activism. I demonstrated at People's Park and the Third World Liberation Strike. We were the radical counterculture. Our bodies were balanced between adrenaline and narcotics. We felt it was our duty to oppose a system that seemed racist, sexist, and exploitative. We had already taken over a great deal of the culture from the grown-ups. Now we tried to take over their politics.

The weapon I chose was the media. My outlet was Dispatch News Service, an anti-war organization dedicated to the publication of articles about what was really going on in Vietnam. The media maelstrom consumed my interests and eventually swept me away from graduate school. I became part of the underground press and moved to Washington, DC.

In Washington I met Seymour Hersh and my life changed forever. We both felt strongly about the war, and when Sy was tipped off to the dark horror that was My Lai, we worked together to bring the story to light. It was an exciting adventure, and our exposé shocked the country into taking a long, hard look at the inhumanity the war had brought down on the women and children of Vietnam and its frightening effect on so many young American boys.

I continued my anti-war activities by helping Daniel Ellsberg make the Pentagon papers part of the American consciousness. I got into a heap of trouble with our government and had to flee the country. Luckily, Nixon's government was even more inept than I was and I was able to return home without being incarcerated.

On the floor of the 1972 Republican convention I stared, slack-jawed, at the forty-foot screen of Nixon's face and decided to dedicate my life to the Movement. I moved back West and became an editor of the radical left *Ramparts* magazine. Imagine my surprise when, only a few months after I started the job, I found out that the Movement was over.

Luckily, I had also learned a new profession—the book business. Two young reporters, Carl Bernstein and Bob Woodward, asked me to help them with a story they were covering: Watergate.

Suddenly I was in the big leagues. I continued to thrive in the book business as agent and publisher of a number of best-sellers. I had become part of the system. As more money and fame continued to pour in, I tried to make sense of what had happened to me and to my whole generation.

How the grandson of a Russian immigrant could become an agent for the grandson of a president of the United States and a friend of the current president is the story of what makes America such a special and unique country. Never before in recorded history has the experiment in social mobility been so successful.

During this period the media irreparably changed the shape of American politics. When I first entered journalism, reporters were still, for the most part, blue-collar workers. Primarily male, journalists were content to cover their beats, come to bat for the paper, and occasionally get a solid hit. After My Lai, the Pentagon papers, and *All the President's Men,* virtually every kid who came into the field was swinging for the fences. "Gotcha" journalism was on all of their minds: the chance to hit the ball out of the park. The chance to get rich and famous. The chance to have a movie star play them on the big screen.

For years baby boomers were defined as those kids born from the time the Second World War ended, all the way through to the middle of the 1960s. I think this is too broad a category for us.

Baby boomers, I think, fall into two distinct categories: early boomers and late boomers. Although connected by their sharp demarcation from previous generations, they are still completely separate animals. The early boomers were, of course, the elder brothers and sisters. The late boomers, for the most part, emulated the cultural breaks the older kids made, occasionally fine-tuning them, but mostly just aping the dress, behaviors, and culture of the early boomers.

Okay, how do you know if you're an early or late boomer, or even a boomer at all?

Some Questions to See What Kind of Boomer You Are

1. While in grammar school, did you or an older sibling personally know anyone who had polio?

2. Did the Cuban missile crisis scare the living daylights out of you?

3. Were you a virgin when you graduated from high school?

4. Did your family become sickened by the way you groomed and dressed yourself?

5. Did you at one time think you could "smile on your brother and love one another right now?"

6. Did you honestly feel that you would live a better life than your parents?

Answers

EARLY BOOMERS = EB; LATE BOOMERS = LB

1. Jonas Salk first got his polio vaccine into schools in 1955. Most EBs would likely have known of someone, probably older, who had contracted the dreaded disease. Fear of living in an iron

lung was big with EBs. By the time most LBs got to school, polio had been eradicated.

2. EBs were old enough to be scared out of their wits by the two superpowers tiptoeing to the edge of nuclear confrontation. LBs kind of knew something bad was going on then because a lot of their great afternoon cartoon programs were preempted by newscasts.

3. The pill! Most EB women couldn't avail themselves of it until after high school and thus graduated chaste. (At least all the ones that would go out with me.) By the mid-60s a sexual revolution had resulted in girls saying yes to boys with a pulse and sexual experimentation had permeated down to the high school level.

4. Both EBs and LBs probably were able to get a rise out of their folks due to long hair, freakish clothing, and a genuinely slovenly attitude. EBs, however, faced the brunt of it, and by the time LBs let their "freak flags" fly, most grown-ups had given up.

5. "Flower power" peaked with the summer of love in 1967. EBs, for a brief shining moment, truly believed we were all brothers and sisters, but such events as Altamont, the Manson murders, and the Chicago Democratic convention slammed it shut. LBs adopted the accoutrements of that movement, but weren't nearly as naive and trusting.

6. Early boomers seem to be the last American generation who truly believed they would live better than their parents. The late boomers have mixed opinions on the subject and those born after 1968 seem to think they'll not be able to equal either the economic or social satisfaction enjoyed by their parents.

The *Homo erectus* stage of human development, that point in history when our ancestors began to closely resemble modern humans, took place roughly 1.7 million years ago. By about half a million years ago we diverged from that to the more familiar *Homo sapiens.* So, roughly one hundred thousand generations of humans lived before us baby boomers. More change will take place during the course of our lifetimes than in all one hundred thousand of those previous generations combined. By the time most of us check out, sometime around 2025 or so, the world will be a far different planet than it was when we found it. The future will be a race between the sustainability of resources, the population explosion, and our ability to deal with the poor on one hand and the expansion of the global brain on the other. If we are foolish, selfish, or narrow-minded in the choices we make, our future may indeed become the apocalyptic nightmare so often portrayed by the current media. However, we also have the possibility of creating a world that will be a fantastically interesting place to live. A world of information and convenience, a world far better than the one we know today. We baby boomers will be the ones who ultimately shape that world. To understand where our world is going, one must understand us and where we have come from. That's what *Too Good To Be Forgotten* is about. I hope you enjoy reading it as much as I enjoyed living it.

CAMBRIDGE

JUNE 1971

There comes a time in every man's life
and I've had many of them . . .
CASEY STENGEL

The guy sitting next to me on the flight from Los Angeles to Boston was either exceedingly friendly, gay, or an FBI agent. He hadn't stopped talking or asking questions since we'd lifted off from LAX. Even after deplaning he had stayed with me, and it was time to claim the footlocker. If he was going to make his move, it would be now. I cautiously approached the special baggage claim window and—no ticket. I had lost my claim stub!

Frantic, I rifled through all my pockets. No claim check and no ticket. Had he stolen it? Was that really a nap I'd taken on the flight or had I been drugged? Was it my imagination or was that a knowing smile he had on his face?

I backed slowly away from him and broke into a run. The man started after me but stopped. I made a mad dash toward the gate. I looked over my shoulder, but he wasn't following me. I made it to the gate and, highly agitated, convinced the ticket agent to let me back onto the plane.

There it was, on the floor at my seat. My ticket and claim stub. A stub for a footlocker stuffed full of documents the United States Supreme Court would hear about the very next day.

I walked back to baggage claim. The man was gone. As I handed the young attendant my stub, I expected to be pounced upon by government agents. I waited to be arrested. The only people who jumped me were redcaps, eager to help with my unwieldy cargo. They loaded the footlocker into a cab and I was off to Cambridge, Massachusetts, to the hotel where I was to meet my contact. I stared out the back window to see if we were being tailed.

I was hiding out. Only one man in the world knew why I'd come here, and he'd gone underground. My life quickly changed from abject excitement to pure boredom. After eighty hours in the same hotel room at the Charles Hotel I had received no calls, no messages, nothing.

These were the days before cable television, and one can only watch so many episodes of *All in the Family* and *Columbo* without losing one's mind. The radio was no better. Every station in Boston was either playing "Theme from Shaft," "Country Road," or "It's Too Late." One station kept playing the entire A side of Carole King's *Tapestry* over and over. (All King! All the Time!) I had to do something.

I glanced yet again at the huge marine footlocker with the cheap metal lock. Kind of a pathetic last line of defense for such important material—but, then again, so was I.

The footlocker belonged to Dr. Daniel Ellsberg, and inside it were copies of *The History of the U.S. Decision-making Process on Vietnam Policy*, better known as the Pentagon papers. They had been published the previous Sunday in the *New York Times* and had caused a national uproar. The Nixon government had immediately gone to federal court and been granted an injunction against the *Times*. The case was now before the Supreme Court. In the meantime, nobody in the world was allowed to read the papers, but here I was, one thin sheet of wood away from them.

I walked over to the table where the remains of my room service lunch sat, picked up a knife, and headed back to the footlocker. I began playing with the lock. It took me about two hours, but I did it! I jimmied the lock. Slowly I opened the lid to the locker.

For the next day and a half I was no longer bored. The Pentagon papers were fascinating, albeit depressing, reading, but there was something else in that locker that blew me away. It was another official document that Dan must have taken, a National Security Council memorandum. In it, the Joint Chiefs of Staff argued about acceptable rates of megakill (one million civilian deaths) that would occur in a nuclear exchange with Russia. As I read the document a familiar feeling began to wash over me—one of pure dread. What these men were calmly debating was my worst nightmare as a kid come true.

Youth

CULVER CITY

The world, dear Agnes, is a strange affair . . .
MOLIÈRE

"DROP!" screamed the public address system in my seventh-grade classroom. All twenty-five of my classmates dutifully hit the floor. I stayed in my seat. Mr. Kargle, my crew-cut, gum-chewing American history teacher, looked over at me and pointed toward the floor. I sadly shook my head. Not today, thanks, I couldn't do this anymore.

We were having a drop drill, one of those genius ideas that some civil defense administrator in Washington had come up with. Civil defense was big that year. Everyone was into it. The backyard bomb shelter business was booming. President Eisenhower had even asked his top civil defense guy to sit in on meetings of the cabinet and National Security Council.

A drop drill was pretty simple. Some grown-up yelled "DROP!" and all us kids were supposed to immediately crawl under our desks, put our heads in our hands, close our eyes, and, I guess, wait for the nuclear firestorm to safely pass over us. It was actually fun the first couple of times (once I even got to see up Susan Quinlin's dress), but I didn't want to drop any more. It scared me.

Today's drop drill was a special one; in fact it was the mother of all drop drills. It was part of Operation Alert, a civil defense test that was being run nationwide. Mock hydrogen bomb attacks were hitting half the country simultaneously. Culver City was one of the lucky cities targeted.

Kargel glared at me. "Get under your desk, David."

I continued to stay in my seat.

"Don't you know that apathy and confusion is what the enemy is counting on?"

I was pretty sure that my staying in my seat wasn't going to tip the balance in a nuclear confrontation with the Soviets.

"You either drop or you're going to give me five miles, Obst!" Kargle snarled. He was also my gym coach and could, with the authority vested in that high office, force me to do anything he wished. I sat frozen for a beat, then decided the actual horror of twenty laps was worse than the theoretical horror of nuclear anni-hilation. I surrendered and dropped.

As I lay there under my desk, I mumbled to my best friend, Alan "It is dangerous to be right when the government is wrong." (I'd just discovered Voltaire.) He shot back, "It's unbecoming for young men to utter maxims." (He'd discovered Aristotle.)

I waited there for the all clear, thinking about the article I'd looked up in the library during lunch. (Operation Alert had done its job . . . I was now alerted to the fact that I was never more than half an hour away from becoming nuclear toast.) It was an article describing the first nuclear bomb test.

The bomb, a great ball of fire about a mile in diameter chang-ing colors as it kept shooting upward, from deep purple to orange, expanding, growing bigger, rising as it was expand-ing, an elemental force freed from its bonds after being chained for billions of years . . .

There I was, scrunched under my desk, looking up at some for-mer classmate's saved gum, and thinking, freed after billions of

years? Why couldn't they have just waited another hundred years
or so to discover it?

The targeted school was Culver City Junior High. Culver City was
a small-town suburb of Los Angeles (population 35,000) surrounded by other middle- to lower-middle-class suburbs (with the
exception of Beverly Hills). A quiet, peaceful, mostly white
enclave, Culver City was an easy place to grow up. It was not a
hard place to score a loaf of white bread, attend a church service,
or find the streets deserted when *I Love Lucy* was on the air. But it
was a fine place to be a kid.

Culver City was also home to a number of movie studios. MGM,
RKO, Hal Roach, and others had their world headquarters in the
city. Huge lots and sound stages hid behind tall fences. The studios were no big deal for us. A few kids had dads who worked
there. But they were mostly below-the-line kinds of guys—grips,
set directors, electricians, and so forth. The stars' kids went to private schools or Beverly High. I didn't know about things like that
at the time.

Unaware of the many cultures surrounding them, the Chinese
considered their land to be the center of the universe. Like the Chinese, I thought Culver City constituted the whole of civilization,
that all things under heaven resided there. I might have been right.

CULVER CITY

JANUARY 5, 1946 (I'M BORN)

Paradise is where I am . . .
VOLTAIRE

My parents, Ray and Goldie, were both recent transplants. My father had been stationed in Los Angeles during the war and had met my mother at a USO dance. That two second-generation Americans, one from the Bronx, one from Minneapolis, should find each other and fall in love in L.A. was a virtual statistical impossibility, but that's what makes horse races . . . and babies.

Their first dance together was to the tune of "Don't Fence Me In" and then to the other top hit of 1945, "I'll Walk Alone." That kind of musical karma might have intimidated some people, but not my folks. By the end of the evening Ray had decided that he was going to court Goldie. Since he only had a few months—he was going to be shipped overseas—he had to work fast. So he did the only logical thing. He followed her home and moved in.

He didn't actually get to shack up with Goldie—she had three other roommates—but he did take over the couch in her apartment. From there he could woo her at close quarters, and, sure enough, a month or so later they were hitched. I've always loved that term. I heard it first at the Culver Theater, a place where, every Saturday morning, you could see two movies, a cartoon, a newsreel, and coming attractions for a quarter. Anyway, some big handsome cowboy sauntered up to a prim-looking cowgirl, rubbed

16

his boot in the sand, and mumbled, "You know, when a fella like me falls for a gal like you, well, they ought to get hitched."

My parents got married shortly after D-Day. The night Ike spoke to the troops, he could have been addressing Ray and Goldie. He said, "You are about to embark upon the Great Crusade. Your task will not be an easy one. Let us beseech the blessing of Almighty God upon your great and noble undertaking. God give you strength." They would need it. A month later my mother was pregnant with me.

My dad, a German-speaking Jew who desperately wanted to fight the Nazis, was sent to the Western Pacific island of Okinawa. There he passed the time making greeting cards for the other GIs (he was a very talented commercial artist) and ferreting out die-hard Japanese soldiers who refused to believe they'd lost the war.

Unfortunately he was unable to make it through the war intact: He got wounded in the foot and was sent to an army hospital in Washington State. Meanwhile, my mother gave birth and we moved into a small one-room apartment in downtown L.A. We spent the first six months of my life together, just the two of us, huddled in that tiny room.

Now some Freudians might posit that this would have had some kind of effect on me—that I might have some issues about inter-dependence on women. But I'm proud to say that I've actually been able to live separate and apart from women for almost a full eight months during my first fifty-two years.

When my dad finally came home it was time for my parents to find the American Dream. Ray and Goldie not only fell in love with each other, but with Southern California. No more freezing winters; sunny beaches year-round; good roads; good schools. In short order they had two other kids, my brother Danny and my sister Judy. We moved into a tract house, the first anyone in either of my parents' families had ever owned. They made lifelong friends, helped start a temple, contributed to the community in so many ways . . . and were wonderful parents.

I seem to have come from a functional family. Neither of my parents drank, swore, or fooled around—or at least we didn't know about it. Their only excesses were doting on the three of us and my mother's incessant mah-jongg games.

Not that they didn't have their faults. Goldie, along with a wonderful sense of humor, had inherited a ferocious temper from her father. Indeed, until she was two, my sister Judy thought my father's name was ShutupRay! My mom was also one of the world's laziest cooks. You can imagine my shock and surprise when at age fourteen I found out that potatoes, carrots, and corn didn't grow in boxes.

Goldie loved to read. Before she finally succumbed to Alzheimer's, I can't remember a single day she wasn't curled up with a book. She was also chronically nocturnal. Her idea of a big time was staying up all night reading Michener or Hersey. As a result, she hated getting up in the morning. Despised it, which was a problem because Danny, Judy, and I had this horrible habit of needing to eat before we went off to school.

Not exactly a domestic goddess, Goldie ranked interior decorating and gourmet cooking in the same category as physical fitness—something she had heard about but didn't care to try. She tried to convince us that breakfast was the least important meal of the day. In fact, she told us medical surveys showed that kids who skipped breakfast were lean and thin later in life and thus lived longer. We didn't buy it. We'd seen the food pyramids in school and knew how important that first egg of the day was. For a while she tried to get Ray to fix us breakfast, but the messes he left behind weren't worth it.

I remember when I was in the fifth grade my mom came home from the store all excited. She had come up with a wonderful solution to our problem: the hot plate. She'd simply make us breakfast the night before so we wouldn't bother her in the morning.

The next morning I wandered into the kitchen and there on the counter breakfast awaited us. Goldie had made pancakes the night before and left them on the hot plate. Not a good idea. They were now about the size of small black marbles and had just about the same consistency. I neatly arranged them on the plate so they spelled out MOM and left for school. The next day the hot plate was gone.

A Jewish mother extraordinaire, Goldie, to paraphrase Will Rogers, never met a baby she didn't like. Whenever she saw a kid, be it at the market or on the street, she would break into that wonderful grin of hers, leave whatever she was doing, and make a bee-line for the kid. Plenty of small children must have turned to their mothers after Goldie left and asked: Who was that crazy lady? And what's a *shayna medala* [Yiddish for beautiful face]?

Our house was a cross between a clubhouse and a hotel. Any out-of-town relatives knew they had bed and board for as long as they wished. Any friend of ours could drop in and hang out. Goldie loved having people around; she fed off their energy and had that amazing knack of making whoever she was with feel like they were the center of the universe. I was fortunate to have had this benevolent soul as my mother.

Ray was an equally exceptional man. His generosity of spirit, eternal optimism, dogged stick-to-itiveness, and broad, corny sense of humor made Raymond Obst a man one could not ignore. Losing his own father at a young age, he had had to become the provider for his family, which meant setting aside the pursuit of his true passions: art and social work.

Raymond Obst was a child of the twentieth century. His life paralleled many of the cataclysmic events that helped shape this country. Coming of age during the depression, he tasted the bitter poverty of the 1930s. Volunteering to fight against fascist aggression, he, like millions of others, went to foreign shores to risk his life. And, like millions of others, he was swept up in the post-war economic miracle that helped deliver the greatest increase in standard of living in history.

As a twentieth-century man, however, my father was unique. While living in the most litigious period ever known, Raymond remained free of ever having to deal with lawyers. While divorce and child abandonment statistics set records during his time, he stayed married for over fifty years to the same woman and never became estranged from his children. And finally, while almost his entire generation of contemporaries became obsessed with chasing the dollar, Ray made just enough to live comfortably and continued to work hard, not for money, but for the two great passions in his life: his family and his sense of social commitment.

So, those were my bloodlines: let's see what I did with them.

CULVER CITY

OCTOBER 1957

There is the greatest practical benefit
in making a few failures early in life . . .
T. H. HUXLEY

On October 7, 1957, a beach ball called Sputnik began circling the earth every hour and a half. Launched by the Soviet Union, it was the first satellite to successfully make it into outer space. It issued a continuous beep that became a kind of outer-space raspberry to a generation of Americans who were so very sure of their own national superiority. A few months before, Ford had unleashed the Edsel on America. Things were falling apart, and what better place to start fixing them than in our schools?

I was in the sixth grade and I thought school was just fine. I liked my teachers, the homework wasn't bad. Then Sputnik.

Suddenly my teacher brought this newspaper into class. She read us the following: "Russian pupils go to school six hours a day, six days a week, attending classes 213 days a year compared to a mere 180 in the United States, and have FOUR HOURS of home-work each day."

As one, my classmates and I became staunchly anticommunist.

The point, however, wasn't that we must oppose the Red menace, but that we must work harder . . . oh, and by the way, every boy in the class better start taking science seriously.

If the educator John Dewey had still been around, they would have strung him up from our school's flagpole. How dare he distort a nation's children into believing that thinking begins with interest? Our teacher calmly informed us she was no longer there to amuse or entertain us. No, it was now her sacred duty as an American to help train minds that were going to beat the Soviets. She was going to work us hard so that someday we could shoot the moon.

My friends and I hoped this would all go away, but just before Thanksgiving the goddamn Russians shot off Sputnik II and put a little dog or monkey or something into the cosmos. Now we were really in for it.

Our teacher kept piling on homework. All thoughts of after-school games of hide and seek or kick the can vanished. It was all math homework. Geez. I'd just gotten my first hula hoop (ninety-three cents of hard-earned baby-sitting money) and needed time to practice.

It was almost impossible to get any sympathy from a grown-up. They were just as freaked as our teacher. My friend Alan, who followed these things much more closely than I did, told me that the pressure would be off after Christmas vacation. The United States was going to launch its own Sputnik in a couple of weeks.

I began reading the newspapers (an addiction that would last the next forty years), trying to find any ray of hope that would calm my teacher down. There it was! Front page of the *L.A. Times:* U.S. READY TO FIRE SATELLITE. I brought the paper to class. Maybe she'd reconsider the seemingly impossible amount of homework she'd assigned over the vacation.

I took one look at my teacher and knew I was in trouble. She'd just come in from the teachers' lounge and looked like she was going to faint.

I bravely handed her the *Times*. She looked at it for a moment, dazed, and then snarled, "Is this your idea of a bad joke, David?" She tore the paper into shreds. "See me after class, you've got detention." I sheepishly retreated back to my desk.

Alan was trying not to lose it. "What's going on?" I asked.

Again, for some reason, Alan always knew what was happening. "Our missile blew up. It got about a foot above the launch pad and exploded." He smiled.

Alan was very good in math; he didn't mind the extra homework because he could whip through it. "Our country is the object of scorn and derision throughout the world," he grinned. "We just launched kaputnik."

This being a just world, I was joined in detention by Alan. That same day, our teacher had asked him what he thought Americans might find when they reached the moon. He had answered, "Russians."

CULVER CITY

OCTOBER 1958

Who shall decide when doctors disagree?
ALEXANDER POPE

Poliomyelitis, also known as infantile paralysis but called polio by all of us kids, was the most dreaded disease around. It seemed like everyone had an older brother or sister or cousin who'd caught it. These older kids all seemed to have severe limps, lived in iron lungs, or died.

Nobody was sure how you got polio, and traumatized parents went to extreme lengths to protect their children. I had one friend whose folks wouldn't let him eat applesauce. Another wasn't ever allowed to swim in a public pool. Alan's parents wouldn't let him go to YMCA camp because they'd heard it was a breeding ground for the virus. The only thing we all knew for sure was that it attacked kids and if you got it you were finished. Then came Dr. Jonas Salk.

Salk, the great immunologist, invented a vaccine that would protect us. In 1955 it was released for use in public schools throughout the country. That was the good news. The bad news was that to take it, you had to get a shot.

The year before, I had lined up with my entire class in front of the nurse's office and waited my turn to be stuck. It hurt. Worse than the pain, however, was the anticipation.

24

They announced our class would receive the vaccination in ten days. Immediately rumors began flying. Dave, one of the smart kids, said that this year they had changed the formula and the shots were killers. "You won't be able to move your arm for two days," he stated with absolute certainty.

This was not good. Kids began to invent graphic horror stories about shot day. My friend Mark swore he'd heard about a kid who fell over in a dead faint after the shot. The goddamn needle had gone all the way through the kid's arm. Every time I would look over at Alan in class he would rub his arm and make moaning sounds. I had to do something.

One of the gifts that I'd been endowed with was the ability to feign illness. Each fall, just as the World Series was about to begin, I'd become afflicted with excruciating ailments. Stomachaches, coughs, sore throats. I was lucky to have enough strength to turn on the TV to watch the games.

On shot day I awoke with what I was certain was a mild fever. I also had a hacking cough, an upset stomach, chills, and a touch of asthma. This was one camper who'd best stay in bed all day.

My mother was already in a foul mood that morning. She was trying to lose weight again and was taking this stuff called Metrecal. Instead of eating, she had to drink a glass of what looked and tasted like chocolate chalk. "Fine, you don't have to go to school," was all she said, and she left the room. Yes! (Being a preteen, it never occurred to me that getting polio would be a far greater misery than suffering the ache of a shot.)

An hour later I was contentedly watching a local TV show called *Engineer Bill*. My mom came in and tossed my clothes on the couch. "Get dressed, we're going to the doctor." Huh? She gave me the "go ahead, say one more word and see what happens to you" look and left the room. I knew I was dead.

The doctor—big surprise—couldn't seem to find anything wrong with me. My mother smiled and casually mentioned to him that this was polio vaccine day at the school. "Perhaps David could get his shot here?"

She dropped me off at school during lunch hour. I looked around for Alan, rubbing my sore arm. He was playing tetherball, smashing the ball around the pole with both hands. "Hey, doesn't your arm hurt?" I asked. He shook his head, trying to get the ball wound around the pole.

"How come? Mine does," I said. He looked at me for a beat and then understood everything.

"We didn't get shots, you idiot. They give the vaccine in a sugar cube now," Alan laughed. I had been an imbecile, and for the rest of the day paid the price as each of my friends took turns punching me in my shot arm. I didn't mind. I kind of felt like I deserved it.

CULVER CITY

OCTOBER 1959

May you live all the days of your life . . .
JONATHAN SWIFT

Nuclear weapons derive their power from the energy released when a heavy nucleus is divided, called fission, or when light nuclei are forced together, called fusion.

I sat back, put my pen down, and sighed, waiting for the siren.

The destructive effects of a nuclear explosion result not only from the heat and pressure generated by the initial reaction but also from release of nuclear radiation.

I had to stop reading this stuff, but I couldn't keep away from it.

An air-detonated weapon produces shock waves that kill anything in its path within a five-mile radius.

For about the hundredth time I calculated how far I lived from City Hall, the obvious target. Our house was still well within five miles.

Nuclear radiation is more pervasive. It is harmful to most organisms, and prolonged exposure is usually fatal.

I glanced over at my dog-eared copy of John Hersey's *Hiroshima*. Two more minutes. I gathered my stuff up and walked out of the library. It was time to go to my next class, Boy's Glee, where I faced the crisis of late puberty.

That week we were singing "You've Got to Have Heart" from the musical *Damn Yankees.* For some perverse reason my teacher had given me a solo on the line "There's nothing to it but to do it." Trapped in my adolescent body was a set of very boyish vocal chords. Each time I sang the fateful line, the class would go into hysterics. No matter how hard I tried to deepen my voice, I still sounded like Doris Day.

In Culver City on the last day of each month, at twelve noon, they tested the air-raid sirens. In Culver City on the last day of each month, at twelve noon, I was sure I was going to die in a nuclear holocaust. Sure enough, just as the school's noon bell rang, the sirens went off. I stood in the hallway for a beat, the familiar feeling of dread washing over me. Screw this. I put my books in my locker and went home.

There was nobody there. I crawled into my bed and pulled the sheets up over my head. I was still there when my brother got home from school. He ignored me, grabbed his mitt, and left the room. An hour later my mom got home. She came into my room and found me between the sheets. She asked me if I was sick and I shook my head. She felt my forehead, shrugged, and left the room. A couple hours later my dad came in to tell me dinner was ready. Again I shook my head. He asked me what was wrong and I shook my head. He left to get my mother.

Now I had the whole family in the room. My brother and sister were trying to figure out what I was up to. So was I. My mother asked what was wrong. I shook my head again. My dad tried to get me out of bed by telling me I was ruining my mom's dinner. This caused Danny and Judy to crack up. It was Tuesday, fish stick night, and we all knew there was nothing you could do to spoil that.

"Okay, suit yourself," my mom said, and they all left my room.

I stayed in bed the rest of the night. Fortunately, I had hidden a number of half-eaten cans of fruit cocktail and some crackers under my bed, so I didn't go to sleep hungry. (The food was left over from an earlier fantasy. I'd made believe that I was a marine, stranded on a lonely atoll, watching for an enemy invasion fleet. Part of the game was to make my scant provisions last until help came.)

The next morning my mother came in to get me up for school. I looked at her sadly and shook my head. She pivoted sharply and headed out of the room. "RAY!" she shouted. "Get in here." Eventually, I spoke again, to my parents, my friends, the school's vice principal, even our rabbi. I told them all the same thing: that since we were all going to be either incinerated in a nuclear firestorm or eaten alive by radiation, there was no sense in doing anything. My logic seemed impeccable—at least to me.

For the next two months I was unmovable. Nobody could convince me that it *wasn't* only a matter of time until the nuclear barrage would come, making life a futile waste. Since nothing mattered, I might as well just stay in bed. I began to fall seriously behind in my schoolwork, which caused further panic and perpetuated my state of paralysis. I didn't realize it at the time, but I was having some kind of a nervous breakdown.

Jung once said, "Show me a sane man and I'll cure him for you." My parents began taking me to a child psychiatrist. I didn't mind; it was better than going to school.

Nothing came of our sessions. I stayed in bed. (My mom wouldn't let me read or watch TV.) A couple of times they made me go to school, but I'd simply walk in the front gate and walk out the back and come back home.

My only outlet was sending away for *National Geographic* travel brochures. Each day the mail would bring wonderful color cata-

logues of scenic Flint, Michigan, or invitations to come visit pic-
turesque Manitoba. I'd file them away—I wasn't sure what for.

Then, one morning, I got a pamphlet from some resort near the
Grand Canyon. It looked so beautiful and peaceful. I started to
cry. I cried for a long time. Then, I got out of bed, washed my face,
got dressed, and went back to school.

CULVER CITY

OCTOBER 1962

A heap of stirring and no biscuits . . .
OLD SOUTHERN SAYING

I never fully recovered from missing those two months. Hopelessly behind in my schoolwork, I not only never caught up, I gave up. My grades tumbled. My attitude toward learning suffered, and worst of all, I became intimidated. Frightened of writing. Terrified that I hadn't learned the rules to adequately express myself (the two months I'd missed were devoted to grammar). Worse, I was now considered an oddball. The guy who lost his mind. I had violated the iron rule of teenagehood: I stood out.

Prior to my "bout," as my mother cheerfully called it, I had steadfastly adhered to the Hobbesian principal that a human's primary instinct is to avoid pain. I was successful in accomplishing this goal at school by the simple act of pretending to be invisible. This had been an effective, albeit lonely, strategy in that it not only kept me from ever being called on in class, it also kept me from getting beaten up. This was an important consideration in the lower-middle-class school world I inhabited.

At Culver, the too-often-abused sons of blue-collar workers would act out their fears and aggression on the frailer members of the tribe. Or, to quote Herbert Spencer, "We have unmistakable proof that throughout all past time, there has been a ceaseless

31

devouring of the weak by the strong." To be invisible was to survive. Now I had blown my cover.

My new strategy was to make 'em laugh. It worked, and I survived my childhood. I agree with Fran Lebowitz that being unpopular in high school is not just cause for doing a book. One story, though.

Seven Days That Shook My World

MONDAY, OCTOBER 22

Jill was way out of my league. Girls' League vice president, pompom girl, great personality, amazing figure. I had watched Jill from afar since the sixth grade. I'd seen both her mind and body grow. She had become that most extraordinary of suburban American creatures: well rounded.

Jill had a marvelous social gyroscope. She was the first girl I knew who referred to herself as a woman. She was the first white person I knew who talked openly about the plight of the Negro. A lot of other kids mouthed off about social issues, but nobody listened to them, while Jill commanded attention. She had been blessed with that most valuable of adolescent treasures: the gift of popularity.

A brilliant student, she was looking forward to college. No "Ph.T." (Putting Husband Through) for her. No, she wasn't going to get caught in either the husband or baby trap. The most amazing fact about Jill, however, the thing I just couldn't get over, was that she had finally agreed to go out with me!

I amused her. We had two classes together and I guess she found my absurd view of the world entertaining. Anyway, we'd become friends. Private friends. Culver, like most schools, had a well-defined social hierarchy. Jill was very close to the summit of the popularity pyramid, while I skulked around near its base. It could have hurt Jill socially to have been seen with me; nevertheless, she'd agreed to a study date.

The year before, Jill had signed my yearbook: "The friendship of a woman is always welcome but when the friendship of a man is offered it means so much. May you truly have everything you want from life. Lovingly, Jill." All I wanted from life was her!

Alan thought I was nuts. I'd shown him the yearbook and he'd said, "Yeah, great . . . it's the kind of note a girl gives her younger brother. Forget it, you have no—excuse me, let me amend that— you have less than zero chance of scoring with this girl." "Woman," I corrected.

That very Monday, at four in afternoon, John F. Kennedy preempted all television broadcasting. Looking damn serious, he stared out at the country and spoke.

Good evening, my fellow citizens. The government, as promised, has maintained the closest surveillance of the Soviet military buildup on the island of Cuba. Within the past week, unmistakable evidence has established the fact that a series of offensive missile sites is now in preparation on that imprisoned island. The purpose of these bases can be none other than to provide a nuclear strike capability against the Western Hemisphere.

This was a double whammy. My worst fears of nuclear annihilation were about to be realized, but worse: What about my date with Jill?

As I listened, in a daze, to the president talk about unswerving objectives and quarantines and so forth, the phone rang. It was Jill.

She was as freaked as I was. She thought we'd better stay home tonight. This was a time to be with family. "Sure," I said.

I put down the phone and walked back to the TV. Suddenly, like a body blow to the soul, it hit me . . . my God, I'm going to die a virgin!

TUESDAY, OCTOBER 23

The next day at school everyone looked and acted as I had in the eighth grade, like they going to die in World War III.

Jill, her golden future suddenly in doubt, was particularly upset. This was not at all fair. Then, an amazing thing happened . . . she became addicted to me.

Maybe it was because I'd been thinking about this predicament for so long it no longer scared me to death, or maybe it was just because Jill brought out the best in me, but I was like a rock for her. Comforting, optimistic, confident.

She began spending all her spare time between classes with me. As soon as I got home she was on the phone. "Talk to me. Tell me it's going to be okay," she pleaded.

I read her a telegram I'd seen in the paper. It was from Bertrand Russell, the Nobel laureate and pacifist scholar, to President Kennedy: YOUR ACTION DESPERATE . . . NO CONCEIVABLE JUSTIFICATION. WE WILL NOT HAVE MASS MURDER . . . END THIS MADNESS. Jill started to cry. I told her I wished I was there to hold her. She moaned.

The world might be coming to an end, but I'd never been happier in my life.

WEDNESDAY, OCTOBER 24

The blockade line was drawn. Cuba was surrounded by the American fleet. Soviet ships were bearing down on the Americans. Meanwhile, our intelligence reports showed that feverish work continued on Soviet missile sites.

I couldn't wait to tell Jill. I rushed to school and found her in the hallway. I put my arm around her and softly explained that if Khrushchev sent his boats through the blockade it might mean war. "This could be our last sunset . . . would you like to watch it with me on the beach?" She sighed and nodded okay.

"What are you doing?" Alan demanded. "You've been waiting for nuclear Armageddon since you were a little kid and now all you can think about is this dumb girl?"

"Woman," I replied. "And she's not dumb."

I borrowed my mother's car. We sat, looking out at the Pacific ocean, listening to the radio. I had one arm around Jill and she had her head on my shoulder. I kind of wanted to change the station to find some make-out music, but there was nothing on but news.

Suddenly a bulletin came across the wires. Twenty Russian ships had stopped dead in the water. Slowly the Soviet fleet began to turn around; they weren't going to try and run the blockade.

In the White House, Secretary of State Dean Rusk turned to National Security Advisor McGeorge Bundy and said, "We're eyeball to eyeball and I think the other fellow just blinked."

In my car, Jill gave me the biggest and deepest kiss I'd ever had. I too blinked.

THURSDAY, OCTOBER 25

The crisis was far from over, but it was beginning to look like there was some hope for a peaceful resolution. Jill was still pretty shaken up, but the adrenaline rush was starting to wear off. My window of opportunity was narrowing. I boldly asked her to come over to my house after school. She accepted.

Thank God, nobody was home. We cuddled up on the couch and watched the crisis.

Adlai Stevenson, America's ambassador to the United Nations, was on live television being asked by some Soviet slimeball to produce proof that the missiles were really in Cuba. I'd always adored

Adlai. A couple years before, during the 1960 Democratic convention, I'd helped push a giant paper ball with a hundred thousand signatures on it demanding his nomination to the front of the Sports Arena in L.A. Anyway, Stevenson whirled on his adversary, demanding he deny that the missiles were there. "Yes or no," he shouted at the Russian. "Don't wait for the translation, yes or no!"

Jill and I were captivated. I kissed her and asked her if she'd like to go out Saturday night. The Russian slinked out of the chamber muttering that he wasn't in an American courtroom. Stevenson pointed at the man and snarled, "You are in the courtroom of world opinion." With that, he pulled back a shroud from an easel in front of him and unveiled blown-up photos of the Cuban missile sites. It was a great moment for America.

Jill turned, kissed me again, and said, "Yes, I'd love to go out Saturday night." Another great moment for America.

FRIDAY, OCTOBER 26

The Cubans were continuing to work like maniacs putting together their silos. Their first missiles would be ready for firing sometime Friday. I just wanted the world to survive until Saturday. At school, people said good-bye for the weekend as if they might not ever see each other again. It was very emotional.

SATURDAY, OCTOBER 27

Three doors down from where I lived, my friend Jeff's father had built a bomb shelter, except that he called it a fallout shelter.

Americans hadn't really needed bomb shelters during World War II. Axis bombers couldn't reach us and the Third Reich's V-1 and V-2 rockets didn't have adequate propulsion to make it to our shores. Now the game had changed. Soviet missiles could target any city in America. Over one hundred thousand shelters were built. Jeff's father's was one of the best.

It was a large, comfortable room with garish green concrete walls, matching pre-AstroTurf plastic carpeting, and a ton of storage space for such useful items as bottled water, canned food, a Sterno stove, a portable radio, and a Geiger counter. There were also a couple of shovels down there so the family could dig out after the war. It was a great place to hang out and, most importantly, it had two huge beds.

Jeff's parents were out of town, back East, visiting his grandmother who was sick. I don't remember what I promised Jeff—probably to do his homework for the rest of the school year or to be his faithful servant to the end of time—but somehow I got him to give me the key to the shelter. It would be the perfect place to take Jill on our date.

Saturday was the day the crisis reached its peak. Reports leaked out that Soviet diplomats in Washington and New York were destroying documents. Both sides seemed to be escalating the conflict. Nobody seemed able to find the off button. The fabric of our world was coming unraveled, and my biggest concern was where I was going to find a rubber.

All my friends had them, circular bulges in their wallets. I knew you were supposed to have them, but I just hadn't gotten around to it. My dad had somehow neglected give me that "special talk" that all teenage boys so look forward to, and I couldn't ask my mom to get them. "No, mom, I'm not really seeing anyone, I just want them to practice with."

Jill and I were going to double-date with my friend Jeff and his girlfriend Jo Anne. Jeff had a great-looking '52 Ford convertible. We'd take the girls for dinner, then go back to his house. My plan was to take Jill into the fallout shelter and talk about the future—or, rather, about the very likely possibility that we had no future.

Okay, my strategy was pretty simple. "Jill," I'd say, "there's a pretty good chance that this is going to be our last night on earth. Do you really want to have lived without ever having made love?" Or something like that.

Jill looked spectacular that night. We sat in Jeff's backseat, holding each other, listening to the news. It wasn't good. Khrushchev had issued some tough statements and didn't look as if he was going to back down. Kennedy had drawn a line in the sand, knowing that if he chickened out he'd probably be impeached. I casually mentioned to Jill that Jeff's dad had a fallout shelter and that it might be a good place to spend the evening. She looked confused.

We were cruising up Sunset Strip when suddenly we spotted these three idiots on the sidewalk wearing Nazi paraphernalia. Jeff had an old Coke bottle on the floor of his car and he tossed it at them, hitting one of the jerks in the back. The Nazis charged the car and Jeff and I were prepared to do battle with them, when, all at once, red lights went on behind us: the police.

We were taken to West Hollywood police headquarters. The desk officer, Lt. Macdonald, called my house, but my mother hung up on him. A nice, considerate son, I always called home if I was going to be late. As I got older, I would try to play games with my mother's head and would disguise my voice. "Ma'am, this is Officer Halloran, we've got your son down here and . . ." Well, sure enough, the policeman began his call to my mom, "Ma'am, this is Officer Macdonald. We've got your son at the West Hollywood police station and . . ." My mother, like most of the country, was glued to her television watching the crisis and didn't want to be bothered. She said, "Leave me alone, David," and hung up.

The officer called Jill's parents, but they weren't home. Jeff's folks, of course, were out of town, and Jo Anne wouldn't give them her parents' number. My plan was falling apart.

They had us sit in a holding cell for about an hour, then called my house again. This time they got my father and my parents rushed down to the station and bailed us out. (We were being charged with disturbing the peace.)

It's pretty hard to do anything with a date in the backseat of your parents' car while being driven home from the police station. But a miracle happened. As we got to Jill's house she leaned over and whispered in my ear that she'd really like to see me tomorrow morning at the bomb shelter.

Back home, my parents didn't know which to be angrier about, the fact that I wasn't listening to their very important lecture or the huge grin on my face.

SUNDAY, OCTOBER 28

This was going to be the most important day of my life.

I woke up at 5 A.M., took my mom's car, and raced over to Jill's. I rang the bell and her mom answered. She gave me a giant hug. Huh? She literally danced with me into the family room. Jill's dad grabbed my hand. He too gave me a hug. Had Jill told them what we were going to do, and were they the hippest parents on the planet? I was just glad I could help out.

Jill jumped off the sofa and came up and hugged me. She kissed my face about a dozen times. This was too good to be true. Finally, Jill pointed at the TV. A commentator beamed at us.

"And so Radio Moscow has now made it official. Premier Khrushchev has chosen caution and peace. The following communiqué was issued this morning: 'In order to eliminate as rapidly as possible the conflict which endangers the cause of peace, the Soviet government has given a new order to dismantle the arms which the United States describe as offensive,

and to crate and return them to the Soviet Union.' After seven of the tensest days mankind has ever known, the crisis is finally over."

Jill and her parents couldn't have been sweeter. They even invited me to go to church with them. I forced a smile and declined.

As I drove home it suddenly occured to me. Fidel Castro and David Obst were probably the two most disappointed men in the Western Hemisphere.

CULVER CITY

MARCH, 1963

It's all right to let yourself go
as long as you let yourself back . . .
MICK JAGGER

Larry was the smartest kid I'd ever met. He appeared to get straight A's effortlessly, was a terrific athlete, lettering in tennis and basketball, and was fairly popular. The best thing about Larry, however, was that he completely got my sense of humor. We sat next to each other in civics and constantly cracked each other up. We were so funny that I almost cost Larry becoming valedictorian because our teacher gave him a B+ out of spite. I got a C− out of pity. (Larry was able to get his grade changed to an A because our history teacher was also the school's American Field Service advisor: that is, he was in charge of our foreign exchange student that year, a girl Alan described as ugly as skunk cabbage. Anyway, Larry volunteered to take her to the Junior-Senior prom and got back his A and his valedictorian honors. Like Rocky said, you gotta do what you gotta do.)

Larry and I became friends outside of class as well. I was a year ahead of him and had a license, so the two of us hung out and participated in that great American teenage pastime, cruising for chicks. We were not terribly successful for several reasons: 1) although we were sophisticated enough not to lean out the window and shout "hubba, hubba" at women, we were both pretty shy, that is to say, still virgins; 2) our cruisemobile was my mother's Chevy

41

station wagon, a car that would have impressed any tradesman needing to lug goods across town, but not a teenage girl with an attitude.

This is not to say we didn't try. With "The Wanderer," "Help Me Rhonda," and "I Love Bread and Butter" blaring, Larry and I roamed the broad avenues of Los Angeles looking for love in all the wrong places. It actually was great fun and Larry's keen wit made it much better. Often times my friends Alan and Marc would join us and on good nights we'd be a regular teenage Algonquin Round Table on wheels.

One night I suggested to Larry that we go down to Marina Del Ray (this was before they developed it) and sniff the red tide. Larry had no idea what I was talking about but shrugged his assent. I rolled up all the windows, turned the air conditioning on full blast, and drove down to the marina. We found an isolated spot near the beach and parked.

The red tide was in; the ocean glowed a fluorescent crimson, an effect caused by billions of tiny plankton feeding near the shore. Along with gremlin hunting, the red tide was the best excuse any of us knew for getting a girl to park at the beach. It was neat to watch, but what really made the red tide special was its smell.

The plankton had this nasty habit of killing most of the small shoreline fish; after a day or two it made for a very interesting odor. That's why I'd closed the windows and pumped up the AC. Larry and I agreed to jump out of the car on the count of three and take as many deep breaths as possible. One . . . Two . . . Three! We both threw open our doors and jumped out. The stench literally knocked us off our feet. The aroma of dead fish was breathtaking. We sucked in as much as we could stand and dove back into the car.

As we drove back toward Culver City, Larry pressed his mouth against the AC vent. Suddenly I spotted them—the Kenney sis-

ters. Larry rolled down the window. "Can we give you a ride somewhere?" Sheila, the older of the two, cracked her gum and snarled,
"How do we know you aren't some kind of weirdos?" This seemed
like a rather stupid question, but Larry was up to it with an
equally half-witted answer.

"Because weirdos wouldn't take you to see the albino farm."
The girls looked at each other for a beat.

"Okay, bitchen," said Sheila, and she and her sister Tina hoped
into my mom's car. I, of course, had never heard of the albino farm,
but after a bit of inane discussion with the beautiful, though none
too clever, Kenney sisters, I realized this was Larry's encoded
message to me to find a dark, secluded place where we could park
and make out. I quickly headed north toward the Santa Monica
mountains to Camp Josepho, my old boy scout camp.

After about half an hour's drive (or five songs on KRLA) we'd
become fast friends with Sheila and Tina. We found out they were
twins, Sheila being the eldest. They were in the tenth grade at
Venice High, and were wrestling with the complex decision of
whether to stay in high school or drop out and go to beauty college.
(Tina confided to me later this was really Sheila's dream; her fantasy was to work in a record store on Sunset Strip.)

We finally arrived at the entrance to Camp Josepho, a dark,
unpaved road leading nowhere. Along the way we had explained
to the girls that albinos were people congenitally deficient in
pigment, with colorless hair and translucent skin. It was obvious
they didn't get it. Larry finally blurted out, "They're real white
folks."

We found a secluded spot and I pulled over and killed the
lights. "Albinos only come out at night because the sun's rays are
too much for them," Larry said. "You can spot them 'cause they've
got bright pink eyes." Tina immediately scooted closer to me.

"They won't hurt us, will they?" she asked in a little girl's voice.

"No," said Larry. "As long as they've been properly fed and we don't make fun of them. If they start to come for us, all we have to do is shine a light on them."

"Do you have a flashlight in the car?" asked Tina.

"Of course," I said. "In fact, just to be safe, I keep a couple of them in the glove compartment. We come up here a lot."

This seemed to console her and soon we were making out. For the next couple of minutes everything went fine.

Suddenly Sheila began screaming. "I see one! I see one!"

Tina broke free of me and dove for the glove compartment. It was empty. "Where are the flashlights!" she shrieked. She began punching me in the arm. "Get us out of here! Drive!!!! C'mon!" In the backseat Sheila continued to howl.

Reluctantly, I started up the car and headed down the road. Suddenly my headlights made contact with a pair of bright red eyes. Larry and I both screamed. I swung the car around and almost drove off a cliff. It was only a white deer, probably out for a night's grazing. I slowed down and calmly drove the girls back to their bus stop.

I wasn't all that disappointed. Tina was a big smoker, and kissing her had kind of been like licking an ashtray. We still had the rest of the night to kill. Larry suggested we visit his friend Derek. We did, and my world was no longer only Culver City.

BRENTWOOD

MARCH 1963

*If this is the best of all possible worlds,
what are the others like?*
VOLTAIRE

Derek was Larry's best friend. The two were by far the brightest kids at Culver. Derek too was on the tennis and basketball teams, was immensely popular, and had the most self-confidence of any boy I'd ever met.

His father was West Coast editor of one of the big Sunday supplements, those kind of tacky magazines that get tucked into your Sunday newspaper. These supplements were powerful, though. With a circulation in the tens of millions, a plug in the supplement could do a lot for a career. As a result, the world beat a path to the editor's door.

Every weekend, the editor and his gracious hostess of a wife were visited by astronauts, movie stars, artists, and politicians. All tried to ingratiate themselves so they could get mentioned in the paper. Derek's father was kind of a modern-day Walter Winchell.

Derek still attended Culver, but his father, now that he could afford it, had fled the lower-middle-class confines of Culver City and moved up the social ladder to Brentwood (about a half mile from O.J.'s). The family's house became our "Hickory Hill," a compound where the brightest and best could play tennis or touch football or just sit around the backyard discussing the events of the day. It was a magical place, heady and intoxicating.

Derek's family was not only a different class from anyone I'd ever known (they didn't have milk cartons or ketchup bottles on the table at dinner), but they had a different mind-set as well. Up to this point I had thought a wine glass was someone who defended the Rosenbergs. Derek's house was a domicile of ideas. The prevailing philosophy was that minds were like parachutes: They only functioned when they were open. Lively discussions on current events took place at each meal. Being around the editor and his family made me want to know more about the planet. They were my window to the outside world. I realized there was so much more to life than what I'd experienced in Culver City, and I wanted a piece of it.

For the boys and girls who hung out at Derek's, being asked to go for a walk on the beach with the editor was the equivalent of being granted an audience with the Pope. I was thrilled when he asked me to accompany him.

As we walked along the shore, the editor went on and on about what our generation could expect in life. He was great with generalities and proverbs. As we walked, he sprinkled maxims in the conversation: "The eggs do not teach the hen," or "The fish dies because it opens its mouth." There was a pause in his monologue. Time for me to speak.

"I've decided to learn Chinese," I said. Where did that come from? I had not given two thoughts to learning Chinese before that moment. I didn't even have a crush on a Chinese girl. Why did I say that?

"Good idea. There's going to be a great need for China scholars once we normalize relations," the editor replied.

Yes! I got approval from the old man!

"Yeah, I'd kind of like to go over there and study. I think the best way to learn about the culture is to live in it," I continued.

"Well, you probably can't get into mainland China, but you could go to Taiwan," he answered.

"Good idea. I'll check out how I can do that."

He nodded his head. He liked this idea. It would be good to have one of his protégés speak Chinese. The editor was very encouraging.

For the next couple of weeks, anytime I went to the house, he'd press me on how my Chinese studies program was going. Suddenly it had become a joke. I was the funny one. Imagine David becoming a scholar?

Well, I showed them. I got into one of the California State Universities and got accepted into their program in Taiwan. I was to leave in the fall. What had I done?

BRENTWOOD

AUGUST 1965

There is always one moment in childhood
when the door opens and lets the future in . . .
GRAHAM GREENE

Derek had a younger sister, Brooke, who was a senior at the very posh Westlake School for girls, a private school attended by Los Angeles' WASP elite. As the sister of a friend, Brooke was off-limits, but her classmates were fair game. One lazy summer afternoon, Derek's college roommate, David, walked out of Brooke's room with her high school yearbook. He smiled and pointed to the book. "Fresh new meat to carve."

David, Derek, and I began leafing through the pages, commenting on the looks and figures of each of her classmates. Looking back, I am astonished at our rampant sexism, but it was sure fun at the time. We narrowed down the girls we wanted to meet to four and approached Brooke for their numbers. She was utterly appalled. For starters:

1. We'd been in her room.
2. We'd rated her girlfriends.
3. We thought anyone in her class would have anything to do with us.

She grabbed her yearbook and left.

David, however, remembered the name of one of the girls, Vivie. Derek got the local phone book and we quickly found her number.

Derek, who even before he went to Yale had had a wonderfully affected preppy accent, snowed young Vivie. Soon we were in her spacious backyard sipping lemonade. Vivie was beautiful, dark, and sophisticated. She was amused at our ineffectual attempts to woo her, and, I think, secretly flattered by our attention. During the first hour or so we were at Vivie's house I spoke in a thick British accent, telling her I was the son of a wealthy English parchment maker. Why I would do something like that is the reason top psychiatrists make a hundred and fifty an hour. Eventually, Vivie politely excused herself to make a phone call. When she came back she told us she'd asked a friend of hers to join us. She said she thought the girl would like us.

Jane Gottlieb was the most striking girl I'd ever met. Tall, tanned, gorgeous, with astonishingly beautiful eyes and a marvelous smile, she was stunning. I turned to David and said, "Dibs."

Falling in love with Jane Gottlieb was the easiest thing I ever did. We connected on every level. We had the same sense of humor, the same absurd view of our parents and childhood, the same passion for finding out about life. In short, we were made for each other.

For the next few weeks I passionately courted Jane. I met her family. Her sister Lynn thought I was cute (if immature), and her parents liked the fact that Jane was finally going out with a nice Jewish boy. In fact, her dad, who was in the construction business, gave me a job working on one of his sites. For the next couple of weeks, I'd proudly show up at the Gottliebs' and display my blisters from digging ditches and entertain the family with my pathetic exploits as a manual laborer.

Our relationship was impeccable but for one small detail—we were both still virgins. The sexual revolution had not yet hit. The pill had not yet transformed America. Eighty-five percent of my high school class had not yet been laid (I hoped). Thus there was a lot of pressure on kids to get it over with. It's no small thing. Sex was still a conundrum to Jane and me. We'd both had a lot of experience trying to figure out the plot line, but for us, the mystery remained unsolved.

Part of the problem was that we simply didn't have any place to do it. We both had siblings at home, so the house was off-limits. Doing it in the car is both unsafe and uncomfortable. The beach has sand and fleas, and so forth and so on. So, even though I was pretty sure that Jane was just as eager as I was to lose it, we were stuck. That is, until Derek and his family decided to go to Europe.

Derek gave me the good news on a Friday. His dad had to do a piece in Paris. I begged Derek to leave his sister's window ajar. "Hey, man, I'm leaving for Taiwan. This is my last chance," I pleaded. Derek said he'd think about it.

Saturday night I picked Jane up and we went to a movie, one of the Bond films. Afterward, I casually drove back to Derek's house, up their long, deserted, driveway. Jane was a bit confused, but she'd gotten used to my peculiar behavior on our dates.

I parked the car, walked around to the back of the house, and looked up. YES!!! He'd done it. The window was slightly open. I raced back to the garage and grabbed a ladder. I passed Jane in the car, waved, and disappeared behind the house. Moments later I came out the back door of the house, holding a can of beer, and invited my incredulous date in for a drink.

Our big moment had finally arrived. We sat in the living room finishing off a six-pack, trying to act relaxed. Neither of us was even remotely comfortable with the situation, but we pretended we were cool. Ultimately, it was time to go upstairs.

I'd like to be able to say that I was a sexual hero, satisfying her every womanly need and desire. I'd also like to be able to say I can play Bach's *Goldberg Variations* and hit a Roger Clemens fastball and bought Microsoft stock in the early nineties . . . but.

awkward 1. *lacking dexterity or skill.* 2. *showing the result of lack of expertness.* 3. *lacking ease or grace.* 4. *lacking the right proportions, size, or harmony of parts.* 5. *lacking social grace and assurance, causing embarrassment.*

Our night was all of the above, especially numbers 4 and 5. We didn't say anything on the ride back to Jane's. I pulled into her driveway, looked sadly at her and said, " 'Night." She got out of the car and nodded. As she walked toward the front door I yelled out, "Hey." She stopped and turned around.

"Jane, you want to try again tomorrow?"

Jane looked at me for a beat, then started laughing. She walked back to the car and gave me a gentle kiss goodnight. I knew I would love her forever.

Over the years Jane and I stayed close friends. Obviously, our relationship had a wonderful sexual tension to it, but we never again tried to recreate that awkward evening. In 1990 I returned to Los Angeles and visited Jane. She had become an artist and her house was full of her new works. I closely examined them, turned to Jane and said, "I love your art . . . actually, Jane, I love you . . . if you don't mind, I'd like to court you." She gave me that wonderful Janey smile, two years later we were married, and we live happily ever after.

Taiwan

*Each generation, like a fine French restaurant, has its own
particular ambiance. Baby boomers, those born between
1946 and 1965, bear a number of truly distinctive character-
istics that set them apart from any other generation. Born
into an era of unprecedented prosperity and inculcated with
the idealism of a limitless future, we grew up believing that
we could change history. Our older siblings had opted for
security. They were detached, determined to succeed—the
Silent Generation.*

*Baby boomers were anything but quiet. Nobody could
accuse these mind-blowing, flower-powered, zonked, past-
blasting psychedelic freaks of being even distant cousins to
the Silent Generation.*

*The two dominant strains of American thought that
influenced the baby boomers were anticommunism and
Kennedy idealism.*

Anticommunism was as close as America came to having a secular religion, and baby boomers were passionately anticommunist. In the 50s, good, red-blooded American boys and girls hated the commies. As we sat eating our TV dinners in the den watching such shows as I Led Three Lives, *we were alerted to the Red menace lurking on the horizon. Problem was, as we boomers got older and smarter, the answers the grown-ups gave us about communism became increasingly absurd. Complex issues were reduced to meaningless simplicities. Our choices were appeasement or war, suicide or surrender, humiliation or holocaust. Red or dead. We opted for none of the above.*

Spokespeople for the extreme right became truly ridiculous. The John Birch Society, the staunchly anticommunist organization that uncovered the government's pernicious plan to undermine our country by putting fluoride in the drinking water, proclaimed: "The whole country is one vast insane asylum and they're letting the worst patients run the place." A spokesman from a wonderful anticommunist group called the Christian Crusade claimed to have proved that the Kremlin had secretly concocted a "Commie-Beatle Pact." He pointed out that "The Communists have contrived an elaborate, calculating and scientific technique directed at rendering a generation of American youth useless through nerve-jamming mental deterioration and retardation . . .

The destructive music of the Beatles reinforces this mental breakdown."

We all gleefully read and watched these pundits with total disdain. Of course, it was only a matter of time until we lumped all grown-ups together and totally disregarded what they had to say. All grown-ups, that is, except one: John F. Kennedy.

The idealism of JFK had a profound effect on our generation. When he declared a torch had been passed to a new generation of Americans, we assumed he meant us. We were stirred by his poetry: "You see things and say, 'Why?' But I dream things that never were and I say, 'Why not?' "

Manned space flight; equal rights for African-Americans; a world well fed and at peace. In following Kennedy's vision we believed we could serve the nation and the truth. All things seemed possible.

I remember the impossible optimism I was filled with in those years. I would proudly boast to any grown-up that would listen that if they didn't destroy the planet, and we got our chance, we were going to settle issues peacefully and sensibly. Or, I carefully pointed out, there would be no generations after us.

Then Kennedy was killed. The country went into a kind of collective mourning. It was like something within us had also been assassinated. Our belief in the future was sadly shaken. We were rudely returned to the present.

In 1965, America was holding onto its innocence by its fingernails. One hundred twenty-five thousand troops were in Vietnam and President Johnson announced that he was doubling the draft call. But, no sweat, the boys will be home for Christmas. Walt Whitman Rostow, the President's national security advisor, assured us that the Vietcong were going to collapse "within weeks. Not months, but weeks." Martin Luther King Jr. and hundreds of others were arrested in Selma, Alabama for the crime of demanding the vote and Malcolm X was shot dead in Harlem. Unsafe at Any Speed *propelled its author, Ralph Nader, into the forefront of consumer advocacy. Nader pointed out that fifty thousand Americans were killed by automobiles each year. Meanwhile, production of soft-top convertibles hit an all-time high, with half a million built that year. The Pop-Tart hit breakfast tables across America and in London tarts began wearing a new six-inch-above-the-knee fashion called the miniskirt. The Rolling Stones burst onto the scene with "I Can't Get No Satisfaction" as the Beatles topped the charts with "Yesterday" and "Michelle." On this side of the Atlantic, Paul Simon and Art Garfunkel had a hit with "The Sound of Silence," as did Sonny and Cher with "I Got You Babe" and Herb Alpert with "A Taste of Honey."*

The top television shows of the year were Bonanza, Gomer Pyle, The Lucy Show, The Beverly Hillbillies, The Fugitive, *and* I Spy. *NBC was the first network to present the evening news in a thirty-minute format, and for the first time all the top shows on network television were in color.*

As I left for Taiwan, America was on a slow simmer. It would not take long for it to reach its boiling point.

TAIPEI

SEPTEMBER 1967

We are what we pretend to be . . .
KURT VONNEGUT JR.

I woke up, looked around, and panicked.

I lay on a small cot in a dormitory at the National Political University in Taipei, Taiwan. The room was about the size of my closet at home. It had a small desk, the bed, my scattered belongings, and me. With a shudder I realized I didn't know a single person within a five-thousand-mile radius and, to compound matters, I was having an asthma attack. It was my first morning in the Orient.

I sat frozen in place. Why couldn't I have just gone to Chinatown to study?

Somehow I made it out of bed and into the street. I wandered, enthralled by the sights and smells of the Chinese.

I watched, fascinated, as an old, bearded man held a cage containing a small rodent in front of another cage holding a deadly-looking snake. The old man lifted a center divider between the two cages and the deadly snake coiled and fired forward. But instead of devouring the terrified rodent, the snake neatly slit itself in half. Buried in the divider was a razor. The old man reached into the cage, lifted out the snake, and deftly removed its liver, which he wrapped and gave to another old man. Whoa . . . we didn't have anything like that at our mall.

By the end of the day I'd forgotten about being homesick and had become a human sponge, absorbing all I could.

Taipei in the 60s was a fascinating city and an urban planner's nightmare. Its filthy streets were crowded with buses and pedi-cabs. Most of the cooking took place outside, using soft coal, and that, combined with the city's location—in a basin—made for the worst smog in Asia. Half of the population was under sixteen and children were everywhere. Open sewers, exhaust fumes, and kids relieving themselves on the side of the road produced an odor that was like no other. The city was noisy, crowded, and dirty. I'd never seen anything like it.

For the past two summers, I'd tutored African-American kids in South Central Los Angeles and had glimpsed one kind of American poverty, but it was nothing like this.

The contrasts were stunning. A shiny, modern Hertz Rent-A-Car office stood by a row of peasant houses made from corrugated tin. Old men sold *shou bing* (a long bun fried in oil and eaten with a sweet bean cake soup) in front of garbage dumps. I seemed to have found the armpit of the world and I loved it.

I settled quickly into a daily routine of intense language study and began making slow but steady progress in my quest to learn Chinese.

I'd never been very good in classroom environments. I had been lucky to make it out of high school with my diploma and fortunate to get into one of the California State Universities. It was their program in Taiwan that I was now attending. My classroom habits hadn't really improved much. My attention would meander from the teacher and I'd begin making lists of my all-time favorite Dodger all-star teams. Instead of classroom notes I'd have complex battle scenes with a myriad of stick figures being bombed by B52s. So, how was I to do something as difficult as learning to speak Chinese? The answer came quite by accident.

TAIPEI

OCTOBER 1967

God help us, for we knew the worst too young!
RUDYARD KIPLING

"HELLO! HELLO!" There must have been about a hundred kids following me down the street, but by now I was used to it. There weren't that many foreigners in Taipei in the 60s. It wasn't a hot tourist spot, and the seeds for the economic miracle that would transform the island kingdom were just being planted, hence not too many businessmen either. Every time I'd venture out, I'd attract a crowd of kids. To them, I guess it was a great free show. They'd never seen anyone with a nose like mine, considerably larger than theirs, and they couldn't get over how much body hair I had. In fact, one of the leading participatory sports on Taiwan was rubbing a *yang gui tze's* (foreign devil's) arm to feel the fuzz. The first few times a couple of little girls began shyly stroking my arm I was somewhat nonplussed, but eventually I got used to it.

As my language skills improved, listening to kids talk about me became a favorite pastime. Once, as I was standing on a crowded bus, two teenage beauties sat in front of me. I listened as they commented on how brutish, repulsive, and hideous I looked. The older one grunted she'd rather be boiled alive than have to kiss a "large-nosed barbarian." When the bus arrived at my stop, I smiled down at the two girls and recited, in my best Chinese, a passage from the *Analects of Confucius* that I had memorized that afternoon.

"When one is not conscientious with one's wishes, one travels along a path of great peril." I bowed and got off the suddenly silent bus.

One day when I was walking home, I had my usual contingent of youngsters trailing after me, laughing, pointing, and staring, when suddenly a baby-faced American teenage boy stopped me on the street. He asked if I spoke any "chink," and when I nodded, he grabbed me and pulled me down the block to the Yeuan Dong Pleasure Palace, a dingy bar. He pushed me inside.

As our eyes adjusted to the darkened, smoky haze, he pointed to a cute, overly made-up girl not much older than ourselves and asked me to propose marriage to her. It was then when I noticed that my farmboy was having great trouble standing upright. He'd been up all night with the girl, a local hooker who worked at the Pleasure Palace, and was out of dough. The girl was ready to move on to her next customer, but our boy, a grunt on a week's rest and recreation furlough and facing the prospect of being back in the Vietnamese rice paddies in forty-eight hours, wasn't ready to call it quits.

I acted as an intermediary, passing along the poor boy's pleas, but was unsuccessful. However, I did try out just about every bit of vocabulary I knew. Even better, the girl was so charmed that I, a long-nosed, hairy barbarian, could speak her language, that she called all the other girls over to listen. It wasn't long before I was the appointed mascot of the Pleasure Palace.

My Chinese improved immeasurably. I became a night person. I'd get up around 6 P.M., study vocabulary for a couple of hours, have breakfast, and head for the bar. I'd spend most of the night with the girls, come back to school for my morning classes, and then sleep all day.

A cheer went up when I'd come into the Palace. (I was like a teenage Norm.) I'd become a *hsiao di* or "little brother" to the bar girls, and it was just as well that they thought of me that way, because I was terrified of them. I mean, I'd hardly ever met a girl who'd slept with a guy and these girls were prostitutes.

The bar was populated with GIs, all of them on R&R from Vietnam. They desperately wanted to communicate with the girls. Most of them had been out in the field for months and were starved for female companionship. They truly appreciated my efforts as a translator. Had I not hated the taste of liquor, I might have drowned in the free booze they offered me. Likewise, the girls seemed to really appreciate my receptive ear, understanding heart, and brotherly vulnerability. I would help them speak with the lovesick soldiers and ultimately became a conduit for some very weird and touching conversations.

TAIPEI

NOVEMBER 1967

We are not about to send American boys nine or ten
thousand miles away from home to do what Asian
boys ought to be doing for themselves . . .
LYNDON BAINES JOHNSON, 1964

By mid-1967 more than seventeen thousand Americans had died
in Vietnam. LBJ had gotten another seventy billion dollars from
Congress to continue the war, and the draft call stood at two hundred thirty thousand men for the year.

I had been reclassified 1-A, but since I was a student in Taiwan
I figured they'd just made a mistake. I wrote them a polite letter
hoping they'd see the error of their ways.

The war was something I dealt with every night at the Palace.
These poor, scared kids would come to the Pleasure Palace and
pour out their hearts to the girls. I heard horrible stories of murder
and mayhem. I began to hear about places called Danang, Cam
Ranh Bay, the Mekong Delta, and Pleiku.

One tall, good-looking guy from Oregon told me how the month
before his unit had been forced to storm a Vietcong stronghold in
the central highlands. His company had taken enormous casualties but had finally secured their objective. A week later they'd
been ordered to pull out. He was sure that the Vietcong had moved
back in and he told me he'd shoot himself in the foot before he'd
go back into action trying to retake the position.

Most of the guys hated the army's standard issue rifle, the M1.
They said it was great for training in the States, but when you got

63

to 'Nam, where it rained every day, it would jam up and was useless. They told me how after every firefight with the North Vietnamese they'd scramble to find the dead enemy's AK47 rifles, the weapons of choice.

The most striking thing about these guys was how hurt they were by the Vietnamese people's reaction to them. They were supposed to be the good guys, so they couldn't understand the apathy and, even worse, the hatred they felt from the native population. Most of them had given up and viewed everyone "in country" simply as "gooks."

Most of the kids I spoke to didn't seem particularly fierce, they just seemed to have had their humanity drained from them.

Most had never been away from home before and had no idea what the war was about. What they did have was the finest weaponry ever invented and orders to kill.

These poor guys, instead of getting to go through the wonderful rituals of becoming men in their hometowns, had Vietnam thrust upon them instead . . . it was a true American tragedy.

HUALIAN

MAY 1967

Eighty percent of success is showing up . . .
WOODY ALLEN

Taiwan, a small island, did not offer much in the way of sight-
seeing, and my budget, roughly $3 a day, precluded travel to any
other place in Asia. I was able to buy a cheap bike and this
afforded me the luxury of leaving the city and spending weekends
in the countryside.

Each Saturday I'd strap my transistor radio to my handlebars,
so I could listen to college football on the Armed Service Network,
and ride deep into the Taiwanese countryside. It was like traveling
in a time machine. Within a few miles I'd be back in Ming dynasty
China. Peasants worked rice fields as they had from time
immemorial. Often, I'd stop and spend time in these small hamlets. The people couldn't have been friendlier. They were as
amazed that a foreigner wanted to hang with them as I was at how
they lived. My language skills were still primitive, but I found
ways to communicate, especially with the children.

On the eastern shore of the island was a fantastic hiking trail
called Toroko Gorge. I decided to check it out. After a harrowing
bus trip from Taipei to Haulian, I took a taxi to the trail mouth of
the gorge. It was spectacular. I tramped about all day. I had never
seen natural formations like those before. Taiwan is a recent geo-

logical uplift, and the sharp, pointed tops of the mountains seemed as if they were from another planet.

After hiking for countless hours into the canyon I suddenly realized there was not enough daylight left for me to make it back out, and this was not a place where I wanted to stumble around in the dark. (I had, of course, neglected to bring a flashlight.) In the distance I saw a small group of houses and made my way toward them to ask for shelter.

What I found was a Jesuit mission run by Father Carl, from Lyon, France. He'd been in China since 1904, had lived in Tibet for thirty years, and had been expelled by the Communists to Taiwan in 1949. His stories about life in Lhasa in the 20s and 30s were so enthralling I could have listened to him all night.

When I returned to Taipei I bought a cheap tape recorder, and two weeks later returned to get Father Carl's stories on tape. I also asked him if there were any other men on the island with stories as good as his. He said that Taiwan was crawling with them, hundreds of Catholic missionaries—Jesuits, Franciscans, Benedictines—all now posted in Taiwan. He even gave me a directory.

I was excited. Nobody had ever bothered to record any of these people's stories. Here was a treasure trove of first-hand observations of what had happened to China during its transformation from a Confucian kingdom to a modern nation-state. In the three hundred years since the West had made contact with China, countless men of the cloth had traveled to the Orient to try and save the "yellow heathen." The Catholic Church in particular committed vast resources to the effort to bring spiritual enlightenment to the Chinese, but the results were disappointing. Some true conversions were made, of course, and the number of "rice Christians" who dutifully showed up at services each morning to be fed swelled the church rosters. For the most part, however, the experiment had failed. The Chinese adhered to their own systems of beliefs. Indeed, more often than not, the missionaries became "sinophiled."

I became fascinated with the whole domain of the missionary experience. I told a friend I'd met in Taipei, another student, about the Fathers and he suggested we contact some universities to see if anyone wanted us to tape the missionaries' stories. We sent letters describing our plan to record the missionaries' experiences to the top twenty colleges in America. Much to my absolute amazement, we immediately heard back from about half of them. Soon they were all bidding for the rights to my tapes. Without knowing it, I had already become an agent.

When the dust settled, Dartmouth, Michigan, and The Hoover Institute of War, Revolution and Peace at Stanford University had become our partners. They sent us what, at the time, seemed like an obscene amount of money, and we were in business.

We divided up the island. Every week I would jump on a plane, bus, or train and track down a new Catholic Father. Some had large churches in Taiwan's major cities, others lived in the mountains with the aborigines, and all had fantastic stories to tell—stories about Mao and the Eighth Route Army marching through their village. Stories about forcing the local warlord not to bind the feet of his daughters, about a China I had only read about in books. These men had not only seen Chinese history, some had even influenced it.

TAI NAN

SEPTEMBER 1967

How oft the sight of means to do ill deeds
makes ill deeds done . . .
SHAKESPEARE, *RICHARD II*

Father Michael was originally from Belgium, but he'd been in China for most of his adult life. His parish was in the southern city of Tai Nan, where he dutifully ministered to a growing flock. I had already interviewed three other Fathers in the area that day and was exhausted when I reached Father Michael's compound, where I would spend the night.

After a modest dinner, we retired to the rectory. Father Michael told me he had been stationed in Southern China. He'd arrived in the early 20s, in the Nationalist capital of Nanking, where he'd taken over a small but thriving congregation. He had been their spiritual leader for almost a decade.

Nanking had a population of about 650,000 people. After war was declared between China and Japan and Japanese soldiers neared the capital, approximately a third of the population fled the city. In December 1937 Japanese troops entered the city. Of the remaining population, all of them noncombatants, close to 300,000 were slaughtered in cold blood. It was known as the rape of Nanking.

For the next two hours, Father Michael told me stories that made me physically ill. He had witnessed war crimes that had virtually no parallel in modern history. He told me how, for the next two months, members of the Japanese Imperial Armed Forces

68

raped and killed any person of Chinese descent they could get their hands on.

The uncle of the Emperor had ordered the troops to kill all captives, and with typical Japanese efficiency, they had tried to do just that.

Father Michael told me how those members of his parish who had remained behind had been promised by the Japanese that if they surrendered peacefully nothing would happen to them. Instead, they were rounded up and systematically exterminated. He told me of walking through the city trying to save Chinese civilians and watching the grisly massacre take place. Japanese soldiers would use men, women, and children for samurai-like decapitation practice. Women from his congregation were raped in his nunnery, and live burials and the roasting of people became everyday occurrences.

My tape had long ago run out and I sat there in tears as he went on and on about the sickening spectacle.

"Couldn't you do anything?" I asked finally.

He smiled. "We tried. There was a German businessman. He'd put on his Nazi swastika armband and go out into the street. He'd try and protect as many Chinese as he could from the Japanese soldiers. We set up a 'safety zone' in the international quarter. We were able to save some . . . but not many."

That night I couldn't sleep. I had just come back from Japan. With the money I'd been given to do the interviews, I'd taken a trip to Kyoto and Tokyo to buy new, high-grade recording equipment. I'd been incredibly impressed by what I'd seen there. Clean, efficient, new—the modern-day Japanese economic miracle was just starting to kick in. I'd written my parents and friends about what a remarkable people the Japanese were. Now this.

As a child, I had been outraged by the horrors of the Third Reich, but I'd only read about them in books. I had no first-hand experience. Father Michael had been there. His accounts, told in his slow, dry, dispassionate European accent, made them all the more chilling. For the first time I understood how easily men could become dehumanized.

At sunrise, I walked out into the church's courtyard with my new tape recorder. Slowly and methodically I began to smash it to pieces. It would be many years before I would again buy anything Japanese.

KAOHSIUNG

SEPTEMBER 1967

*I'm always at a loss to know
how much to believe my own stories . . .*
WASHINGTON IRVING

A few weeks later I had to make another trip south. Between my language studies, hanging out at the Pleasure Palace, and interviewing and transcribing my missionary tapes, I was pretty worn out. And I was lonely. All this would change once I reached Kaohsiung.

I was in Kaohsiung to catch a train back to the capital. The night before, I'd interviewed a Portuguese Father in a remote hill village deep in the central highlands. The good Father's charges were the remnants of an aboriginal tribe (*Shang Di Run*) that was quickly disappearing. As a result of population growth, new roads, and a robust economy, the tribe was being absorbed into the mainstream Taiwanese culture at a rapid pace.

I ate with the tribal elders in their great hall. A huge circular table dominated the room. In the center of the table was a large hole. The food was delicious, although I didn't dare ask what it was.

Proper Chinese dining etiquette differs from ours in one important aspect: No Chinese ever drinks alone. Instead, people offer a toast to one of their culinary companions. The toaster offers two options, *suai bien* (have a sip) or *gam bei* (bottoms up). Since I was the honored guest that night, each of the dozen or so men felt it incumbent to toast me, each with a hearty *gam bei*. Suffice it to say I was totally inebriated before long.

Eventually, a large monkey was brought into the room and placed in the round hole at the center of the table. My companions began to toast the monkey, even giving him a large cup of the potent rice wine to drink from. In no time the monkey was as drunk as I was. Everyone was having a swell time until . . .

The village headman stood and suddenly everyone quieted. He calmly picked up a huge cleaver and stood behind the monkey. I picked up my glass and was about to toast him and the monkey when—THUMP! He brought the cleaver down squarely on top of the poor monkey's head, splitting his skull neatly in half. The headman then deftly removed the monkey's brain, cut off a large slab, and gently placed it in front of me. Suddenly I was quite sober.

I'd like to be able to say it tasted like chicken, but I'd be lying. The fact is, I didn't taste a thing. I had no choice but to eat it; to refuse would have caused the whole village to lose face. I picked up the dripping morsel with my chopsticks, jammed it into my mouth, and prayed it would stay down. It did, and I was still thinking about it the next day.

I had a few hours to kill before my train back to Taipei. I decided to practice some Chinese in my favorite language lab, so I headed to the red-light district where I found a bar full of GIs. I was only there a short while when one of the grunts grabbed me and pulled me outside. He was sufficiently drunk to waive the niceties of asking for my help and instead commanded me to accompany him to a small shop down the block. He wanted to buy some tacky souvenirs for his girl back home. He also desired that I ask the pretty young thing that worked there if she would please go down on him. I helped him with his first request and, fortunately, he became so nostalgic for his sweetheart he forgot about the latter. However, I had now met Yu Lin.

Yu Lin was seventeen, the fourth daughter of a native Taiwanese farmer and beautiful. She had huge, black, expressive eyes filled with a mischievous twinkle.

When the soldier stumbled out of the shop, Yu Lin and I began to chat. Four hours later we were still talking. She asked me if I'd like to see the sights of Kaohsiung—an oxymoron—and after about a nanosecond of consideration I said yes. I'd already missed my train, but figured I could get a cheap room in Kaohsiung and go back to Taipei the next day.

Yu Lin closed up shop and we flagged a cab. As we drove through the port city, she pointed out the sights of her hometown. My Chinese by this time was just good enough to keep up with her running commentary, but it wasn't her words that interested me— it was her attitude (okay, and her body). Yu Lin seemed to be on a perpetual high. Everything made her smile. Her genuine enthusiasm was infectious.

That night we had dinner and it was one of those magical evenings when everything seemed perfect. She dropped me off at a cheap hotel and as I walked her back to the waiting cab I'd never wanted to kiss a girl so much in my life . . . and there's the rub. I hadn't a clue as to what proper etiquette was with a Chinese woman. Would she be insulted if I tried to kiss her? Would she be equally offended if I didn't? Maybe I should . . . Yu Lin settled the issue by grabbing me and giving me a long, tender kiss. She laughed, got in the cab, and drove away. I was smitten.

TAIPEI

OCTOBER 1967

A man in love mistakes a pimple for a dimple . . .
CHINESE PROVERB

I found it incredibly difficult to do anything except think about Yu Lin. She had no phone, so the only way I could communicate with her was by letter. My problem was that at this point in my Chinese studies, my written language skills were still pretty basic.

Written Chinese is a pictographic language. It has no alphabet, and to be considered literate one must memorize close to a thousand characters. These are used in compound structures to make up words. To learn to write Chinese is both difficult and time-consuming. I could almost speak at something approaching a university level, but I wrote like a fourth-grader. And most fourth-graders don't write love letters.

Fortunately I'd made friends with a couple of American expatriates in Taipei. Tom, an ex-marine, had been there for almost three years and was light years ahead of me in language skills. An enthusiastic drinker, he never had any dough. He liked me well enough, but unless I was buying, he didn't spend much time with me.

I tracked Tom down and pleaded with him to help me write a long, romantic letter to Yu Lin. I wanted to invite her to come up to Taipei to visit. He wasn't interested.

Like patriotism, bribery is the last refuge of the scoundrel. I told Tom about my newfound hobby at the Pleasure Palace. I told him he could have my spot. He'd never have to pay for a drink again, if only he'd write the letter for me. He grabbed his writing brush and headed for the door.

We sat in the dim light of the Palace composing the letter. I told him what I wanted to say and Tom reworked it into what he claimed was beautiful Chinese prose. When we finished, he told me we had composed a masterpiece. He read it to the girls at the Yeuan Dong, who squealed with laughter and agreed with Tom that no woman could resist such a letter. They promised me it would win Yu Lin's heart.

In the letter I had invited Yu Lin to come up to Taipei the following Saturday. That morning I put on clean socks for the first time in a week, straightened up my room (which was not too hard to do since you could stand in the middle of the room and touch all four walls), and set off to the train station to meet her.

The train from Kaohsiung was only a half hour late, not bad for Taiwan. I stood at the exit gate, watching the passengers go by and thinking how strange it was that I'd never met any of them. Hundreds, perhaps thousands of people were passing me, and I realized that our whole lives would be lived without our ever knowing each other. This sea of oriental faces, each with their own life, their own history. I snapped myself out of this bizarre train of thought with the sudden realization that I wasn't sure I remembered what Yu Lin looked like. I had this image of her in my mind, but what if . . . ? I needn't have worried. She wasn't on the train. Or the next one. Or the next one. She hadn't come.

In 1967, ceremonies marking the installation of the one hundred millionth telephone in the United States were attended by President Johnson and representatives of the Bell System. Americans had approximately half of all the telephones in the world. Yu Lin didn't have one.

I was going crazy. There was no way to reach her. I laid in my cot each night and suffered. It was intense.

———

I had to do something, so I went back to Kaohsiung. Yu Lin was not at all surprised to see me. In fact, I think she had to fight back a grin. Yu Lin summoned all of the discipline a seventeen-year-old could muster and gave me a reproachful look.

"Why are you here?"

"I had to see you."

"Oh, so you could feel what my soft pomegranate lips taste like? Or maybe softly stroke delicate rose petals across my skin?"

Hey! Those were lines from my letter. Maybe Tom's beautiful Chinese prose hadn't been quite as splendid as the girls in the Pleasure Palace had promised.

Yu Lin reached behind the counter and pulled out my letter.

"This is the kind of letter you write to a prostitute—not a good girl," she said, waving the letter at me.

"So that's why you didn't come to Taipei?"

"I thought you were a smart, funny, nice guy . . . then you write a letter like this. I'm not sure I want to have anything to do with you." She shook her head. "Maybe we're just too different. Maybe we . . ."

I grabbed the letter and tore it up.

"Listen, I didn't really write this letter. I can hardly write my name, let alone a love letter. I had a friend do it for me." I confessed. I grabbed a writing brush and some paper off the counter and wrote my name and some other characters.

Yu Lin came over and looked down at my pathetic calligraphy.

"Are all Americans so stupid?" she asked, smiling.

I smiled back. "No, just the special ones."

TAIPEI

OCTOBER 1967

Be sure you're right—then go ahead . . .
COLONEL DAVID CROCKETT

Yu Lin sat curled up next to me on the train back to Taipei. We'd had a wonderful two days in Kaohsiung. She'd taken the day off and we'd gone to a remote park outside of town and had a picnic. We'd taught each other children's songs in our own languages and I don't think I'd stopped smiling for about forty hours.

I was lying on the blanket in the park, softly singing a Chinese song about a young lady who shouldn't be angry about having to wait a day for a ride on a banana (I may have screwed up the translation) when Yu Lin leaned over and kissed me. I responded, and the next thing I knew, I wasn't a virgin anymore.

As the train pulled into the station and we disembarked, I looked around for Yu Lin's friends or relatives. She had told me she wanted to ride with me back to Taipei, and I assumed she had business or something to do in the capital. I didn't really care. I was just glad she was going to be in the same place.

After about twenty minutes, I turned to Yu Lin and asked her where she wanted to go.

"Why, your house, of course," she replied, giving me a quizzical look.

"My house?"

"You live in Taipei, don't you?"

77

"Yes, but . . ."

"Good. Take me home." She picked up her suitcase and headed for the front of the station. I hurried after her and grabbed her arm.

"But I thought when you said you wanted to ride with me back to Taipei you were . . ." I stammered.

"Running away with you." She smiled. "I've run away from home. I'm going to live with you."

TAIPEI

APRIL 1968

Love is being stupid together . . .
PAUL VALERY

The next seven months were a happy blur. I moved out of my dingy room and got a nice, comfortable place on the outskirts of the city. We started playing house.

Neither of us was quite sure how we were supposed to do this—that is, live together like grown-ups—so we made up our own rules. I was sure I was the luckiest guy in the world.

Yu Lin was that most interesting of creatures—a girl/woman. She could be amazingly mature, taking care of the mundane activities of running a house, but basically, she was still a little girl. One day, on my way home from class, I spotted a large doll in a shop window. I went in and bought it. That night I gave it to Yu Lin. She said it was the most wonderful gift she'd ever received. As a little girl she'd never had a doll. For the next few months, I'd come home and see the strange but remarkable sight of the woman I loved sitting on the floor playing with her doll.

Adages become truisms for a reason, and *The best way to learn Chinese affairs is to have one* was particularly apt. Nothing beats pillow talk. My language skills improved exponentially. I even began to dream in Chinese. It was the best of times.

Given my meager funds, phone calls to the States were out of the question, so I became a voracious correspondent. I'd write home at least once every couple of weeks to let my parents know I was okay and to share my experiences with them. Here is part of the last letter I wrote to them after being away almost two years.

You know, I've never really thanked you for letting me come here. You really have afforded me the opportunity of seeing the world and its peoples and ideas. I hope that with the education and experience I've gained here that maybe some day I can do something about all the misery and unhappiness I see around me.

I wonder if you'll notice a lot of changes in me? I feel like I've gained a little responsibility, a lot of knowledge, picked up some happiness, and a ton of experiences. I know I'm a lot more tolerant of the world's problems.

Anyway, I don't want to sound too corny and I know it's unusual for someone my age to respect his parents (see, that Chinese filial piety stuff is rubbing off on me) but I really do want to thank you for having the faith and courage to let me come halfway 'round the world to grow up. I hope you'll be proud of what your confidence has produced.

Your man in the Orient,
David

TAIPEI

APRIL 1968

I'll get you, my pretty, and your little dog, too . . .
WICKED WITCH OF THE WEST, *THE WIZARD OF OZ*

"Ching hsia lai! Ching hsia lai!" The pounding on our front door startled Yu Lin and I awake. Somebody was screaming something about the police coming? I rushed to the door. Frank Chen, a friend I'd made at the University, stood there panting.

"The police came to the school this morning looking for you! They want Yu Lin," he told us excitedly.

Our worst nightmare had come true.

Yu Lin and I both knew that when she ran away her parents would not take it well. It would bring shame to her family, indeed to her whole village. This was not something a nice girl did. We tried to rationalize our relationship—"love conquers all"—but we both knew that we'd brought a great deal of dishonor to her family.

They hadn't the resources to hire a private detective, and their entreaties to the police had been, for the most part, ignored. There were too many other girls like Yu Lin.

Thousands of American boys were now visiting Taiwan as a result of the Vietnam War. Working in the right bar, a girl could make the equivalent of her father's yearly salary for a good week's activity. Girls were flocking to the city in droves to get a taste of that economic miracle called R&R.

Yu Lin ran to the closet and stuffed her meager belongings into a bag. (She only had a single orange dress.) She and Frank quickly left the house . . . you see, I had a plan.

Ten minutes later, the police did come pounding on my door. They looked around the house and then escorted me to police headquarters.

"Where is she?" asked a short, squat, mean-looking officer I'd mentally named Mutt to differentiate him from his tall, chain-smoking partner, whom I called Jeff.

"Where's who?" I calmly replied.

He turned away trying to control himself. If I'd been Chinese he would have just started belting me until I fessed up, but my being a foreigner made him uneasy.

"You know who!" he screamed in English. I had not responded when they had questioned me in Chinese. I would only speak English to them. This helped, because I could listen to them speak to each other without their knowing I understood them.

"I'm sorry, but I have no idea what you're talking about," I answered as politely as I could. Jeff motioned to the policeman by the door. The man left.

I had no idea why they'd decided to come after us. Maybe Yu Lin's family had found some important official in Kaohsiung to pull strings in the capital? Maybe they were getting nervous about the contents of some of the missionary tapes I had done? Whatever the reason, I seemed to have really pissed these two off.

The policeman returned with a wizened old man, the local dumpling vendor. The man was clearly terrified. At that time Taiwan's legal system didn't include such niceties as habeas corpus or the rights of the accused. In general, if you were picked up by the police you were not only guilty, you were screwed.

Mutt pointed at me and asked if the old man had ever seen me and Yu Lin together. The man quickly nodded.

"Yes, he and the girl are good friends. I see them almost every night."

Mutt pushed the man out of the room.

"He just said he saw you with the girl last night. Now, I'll ask you again, where is she?"

"He must be mistaken. Do you by chance have a picture of this girl? I'd really like to help you," I answered, acting much braver than I felt. Actually, I was scared out of my mind.

Jeff walked over to his partner and pointed at me. He said in Chinese, "Tell him that unless she's in this office by the end of tomorrow he's going to jail for five years."

Mutt smiled and stuck his face right next to mine. "You either bring her back by tomorrow or you're going to jail for ten years!"

"Wait a minute! He said five!" Oops, I had blown my cover.

It didn't matter. They were done with me.

I walked out into the street and felt surprisingly calm. I was kind of glad that things had come to a head. I had a plan.

As I headed back to my place, I noticed two skinny guys in bad suits seemed to be following me. I deliberately turned left a block before my house and, sure enough, so did they. I was being tailed. I guess they figured I'd lead them to Yu Lin. I wasn't sure what I should do. Suddenly, James Bond took over.

One of the joys of living in Taiwan was that I got to see all of the American movies, albeit half a year late, for ten cents. Taiwan didn't sign any of the copyright convention laws, so its citizens were free to rip off the intellectual properties of the world with impunity. I had bought a record player when I arrived and quickly amassed an incredible collection of classical music. Records cost a dime each. The complete nine symphonies of Beethoven cost me two bucks. Anyway, the week before, Yu Lin and I had gone to see the latest Bond film. I decided to try something I'd seen in the movie.

I entered the foyer of a large apartment house and pushed every buzzer on the wall. Sure enough, a couple of people answered and I got buzzed into the building. The two skinny suits ran up to check where I was going, but were stuck outside.

I walked through the lobby and left by the back door. I'd lost my tails. Cool. Now what? I rushed back to the house. The place was a wreck. Someone, probably the police, had gone through all my stuff. I pulled open my desk drawer and all my papers were gone. My passport was missing, and, more importantly, so were my Taiwanese identification papers, a small black booklet used for virtually every financial transaction in the country. Without that book I couldn't withdraw money from the bank or buy a plane or train ticket. Suddenly my plan had sprung a couple of holes.

I dashed out of the apartment and went in search of friends. I found Frank and Tom and made them loan me all the cash they had between them, about two hundred bucks. It was getting late and I had to get to Keelung.

Keelung was a small fishing village on the northeast shore of the island. There I had befriended a wonderful French worker-priest, Father Anthony. He had a small congregation on the coast and spent most of his days fishing and talking about his life in Canton in the 20s. I had interviewed him early on in my project and we'd since become good friends.

My plan with Yu Lin had always been that if anything happened, we'd meet at Anthony's.

I grabbed a cab and spent thirty of my two hundred dollars getting there.

Yu Lin was feeding birds in the courtyard when I arrived. We rushed to each other and hugged. I told her what had happened and she began to cry. I tried to comfort her. Unfortunately, my plan was a bit shortsighted. I had come up with the idea of meeting at Anthony's, but that was kind of the beginning and end of my plan.

Hiding out was not a viable option. Taiwan was a police state. There were over five hundred thousand men in uniform. The chances of a pretty Chinese girl and a foreigner avoiding detection were negligible.

Anthony mentioned that there was historical precedent for the church offering sanctuary, but he was afraid we'd be bored to death staying in his tiny, cramped compound.

"What if we fled the country?" I asked.

"How?" Yu Lin replied. "They've taken your black book, plus they'd never give me a passport."

"No, we could . . ." I jumped up and ran out of the courtyard. I jogged down the beach to where a number of fishermen were working on their nets and boats. I approached a weather-beaten Taiwanese man.

"How much to take us to Hong Kong?" I asked him.

He looked back at me as if I were crazy, which I probably was.

"My boat couldn't make it that far if it had a typhoon blowing it." He laughed. "Plus the patrol. If they caught me . . ." He suddenly started looking around, then motioned for me to leave him alone.

I walked up to another fisherman and repeated my request. This guy had a much better answer. He looked at me for a beat and then ran down the beach.

I sadly walked back to the church.

That night Yu Lin and I slept on the beach. We stayed up most of the evening, talking, crying, holding each other, trying not to lose hope. Just before sunrise she fell asleep. I watched her and tried to imagine what it was going to be like without her.

I shook her awake. "Yu Lin," I said excitedly, "will you marry me?"

TAIPEI

APRIL 1968

There's no such thing as a free lunch . . .
MILTON FRIEDMAN

We carefully hid behind the wall, looking out at one of the prime pieces of real estate in Taipei, the United States embassy.

A marine guard opened the front gate. Yu Lin and I grabbed each other's hands and sprinted as fast as we could across the already crowded main drag of Taipei and dashed into the embassy. Returning to the capital had been frightening; we were sure every policeman and soldier we saw was looking for us. All morning we had hidden in alleyways and back streets waiting for the embassy to open. If we could get inside we'd be safe. We'd be able to stay together.

We rushed to the front desk. Breathing hard, I explained to a bored, officious-looking guy in a three-piece suit that we were in great danger but he could help us out. He barely looked up from his paperwork.

"What do you expect me to do for you?"

"We want to get married."

Finally he looked up and casually checked Yu Lin out.

"How old's the girl?" he asked in a snooty Ivy League accent that made me want to punch him.

"Eighteen," I answered.

He scratched his head, bored and not wanting to be bothered by us.

"Yeah, well, hold on a sec." He spun his chair around, opened a file cabinet, rummaged through it, then handed me a form.

"Just have her parents sign these and come back to see us." He snickered. I'd just told him our story and he knew that wasn't going to happen.

"But—" I was trying not to lose it.

"Hey, I don't make the laws," he sighed. "If you really want to marry this girl," he said the word as if tasting a piece of bad fish, "then you must get her parents' consent."

He gave a weak, shit-eating grin and stood up.

"Now, I really have quite a bit of work to do . . . will there be anything else?"

I put my arm around Yu Lin and walked away. It was all over.

Yu Lin and I walked the three miles across town to the police station, then stood outside holding each other for a long time. I took her in my arms and we looked into each other's eyes. I tried to memorize her soul, but all I could see was a sad, teary-eyed young girl. Finally we had one long, tender kiss goodbye, and went into the police station, and I never saw her again.

CULVER CITY

APRIL 1968

The world is a comedy to those who think,
a tragedy to those who feel . . .
HORACE WALPOLE

I was back at home, sharing a room with my teenage brother. All of my friends were either away at school or halfway around the world. I was miserable.

I'd written countless letters to Yu Lin, but none of them had gotten through. I even tried to send them through friends, but her parents had effectively blocked communication between us. It was sad and frustrating.

Not that I didn't have stuff to look forward to. There was that long-awaited trip to the dentist to correct two years of hygienic neglect. There was filling out applications to graduate school, and, best of all, there was dealing with my draft board.

The Selective Service System required one to notify them, within ten days of its occurrence, of any fact that might change one's classification. I called up and gave them the good news I was home. They gave me the good news that I was still 1-A and that I would probably be drafted within the next two months. This was not a dream come true.

I decided to file an appeal before my local board.

I showed up there not knowing what to expect. I had not yet begun to dress or wear my hair like most of my peers, which must have helped. When I appeared at the hearing in a coat and tie, and with short hair, I apparently didn't push any of the board members' buttons. The other advantage I had was this was a local board. A couple of the sons of the men serving on it had known me all my life.

I told the board that I would refuse to go to Vietnam if drafted. I told them that I believed in my country, but that based on what I'd seen and heard from our troops during my time in Asia, I could not in good conscience participate in the killing. I told them I would be going to graduate school in the fall, and that that didn't really matter, because after I got my degree I would still refuse to go.

One of the board members was obviously disgusted with me, but he served on the local Mental Health Guidance Clinic with my father and had too much respect for Ray to make an example of me. Another tried to persuade me that I couldn't just pick which wars I wanted to fight for my country. He said that it was up to our elected leaders to make those decisions. I reminded him of a statement by George Ball, Kennedy's former undersecretary of state, who'd said that his colleagues were like "a flock of buzzards sitting on a fence, sending the young men to be killed. They ought to be ashamed of themselves." Afterward I felt badly for bringing this up. It must have been a terrible responsibility for these men to send their neighbors' children off to war.

We debated for quite some time. I did not use the rhetoric of the radical left to make my points, as I didn't really know it yet. More importantly, my argument was highly personal. I explained that, having lived in Taiwan, I'd grown to understand and admire the people of Asia. I told the board that I would be a liability to my fellow soldiers in the field because I would find it virtually impossible to hate or want to kill the enemy.

I tried to stay calm and unemotional, which was easy because I really had made up my mind that I would not go. It was the seventh grade all over again.

The hearing ended and the head of the board told me he was disappointed in me as an American. I could live with that. He told me I was fortunate that this board had no trouble meeting its monthly quota of draftees each month. (After all, Culver City was a middle- to lower-middle-class town and not too many guys went to college.) He also told me the board was very busy and didn't want to be bothered by having to deal with me. Finally, he told me that the best they could do was give me was a medical deferment. Was there anything wrong with me?

"Well, I had pretty bad asthma when I was in Taiwan."

He looked at me and frowned.

"Get a letter to us from your doctor," he mumbled and waved me off.

I stood and walked up to the dais to thank the board members. None of them would make eye contact with me and, of course, none of them shook my hand . . . but I was free.

Free to do what, though?

Graduate school wouldn't start until fall, but I didn't want to wait. Derek called from Yale and told me I should meet a really interesting guy on their faculty, Kenneth Scott Latourette, an expert in the field of China and the missionary movement. I should call and set up an appointment.

One of the great things about being young is that nothing intimidates you. I picked up the phone and called Dr. Latourette. I had no idea that he was one of the most distinguished members of the Yale Divinity School's faculty, with the regal title of Sterling Professor of Mission and Oriental History. He had been associated with Yale since 1904, when Teddy Roosevelt was president. Now an emeritus professor, he continued working part-time at the university as a legend in the field of East Asian studies.

Dr. Latourette was now ninety-two; demands on his time were excessive, and he had to budget his days judiciously. Luckily, both his assistants were out when I called, and he answered the phone himself. I told him about the tapes I'd done with the missionaries in Taiwan and he invited me to Yale to discuss them. Two days later I was in New Haven.

For the next two weeks I pretended to go to Yale. I moved into Derek's room with him and his roommate, David. I slept on their couch. Strobe Talbott, who was to marry Derek's sister Brooke and become Bill Clinton's roomate, showed me how to crash the various dining halls and get free meals. Another hometown friend, Jacques Leslie, lent me his library card. They all took very good care of me. For my part, I really loved making believe I was a Yalie. I sat in on classes, attended lectures, went to mixers . . . I was an academic Walter Mitty.

My meetings with Kenneth Scott Latourette (isn't that a perfect name for a scholar?) were more than I could have dreamed. For the first time in my life I received academic validation for something I'd done. He told me the tapes were enormously important and offered me a position working with him at Yale Divinity School in the fall. I was dumbfounded. I'd barely made it out of high school and now I was being asked to go to Yale!

So, what did I do? I glibly replied, "Gee, and folks had so hoped I might go to Harvard." A bad joke . . . especially to a guy who deals with people who go to Harvard every day. He thought I was serious.

Kenneth Scott didn't miss a beat. He looked hurt as he nodded his head. "Of course, I understand. Here, let me dash off a note to my friend John," a reference to John King Fairbank, the director of Harvard's East Asian Research Center and another legend in the field. The top of the food chain. The Mick Jagger of Chinese studies.

Dear John,

This will introduce Mr. David Obst, who is just back from two years in Taiwan and has had interviews in depth with Catholic missionaries from the mainland. From a visit with him I was of the opinion that he has gathered highly valuable material which will be of major importance. I am of the opinion that being of Jewish background he can write from a unique perspective. If you can take the time to direct him, I think Harvard is best place for him to apply.

Always cordially,
Ken

He ruefully handed me the note and moved to stand up. I didn't know what to do. Fortunately, it took Kenneth Scott Latourette a long, long time to get up. I rushed over to him.

"Dr. Latourette? You know, we of the Jewish background have what's known as an ironical sense of humor."

He stared back at me.

"When I said I really wanted to go to Harvard I was joking."

"One really doesn't joke about going to Harvard, does one?" he said.

"No, of course not. Nor do I take your kind offer of my studying here with you as a joke. I would be so honored if . . ."

"No, no. I'm afraid not. I think it best, if you're going to view your education with such levity . . . no, I think it best if you go to Princeton."

I was stunned.

"Princeton, sir?"

"Yes, of course. Everyone knows their Chinese studies department is a joke."

I stood there, my mouth wide open.

Latourette burst out laughing. He actually slapped his knee.

"Got you! You see, you Jews aren't the only ones who can be ironic."

He walked over and held out his hand.

"Thank you for coming in. I'll see you next fall. I look forward to working with you."

Chicago

The America I returned to had undergone profound changes. The most striking was the chasm that now existed between kids and grown-ups. The missile gap had been superseded by the generation gap. Baby boomers and adults truly didn't seem to like one another. What was going on?

Adults were perplexed and confused and fascinated by what had happened to us. Indeed, by the late 60s the whole nation was obsessed with us kids. Why? Because we were rebelling, and that rebellion's every action against the established order was reported with deadly earnestness by the media.

Part of the problem was that, as with the cyber-angst experienced by older people in today's communications revolution, no one wanted to be left behind. The adults knew that something new and fun was going down, and they wanted to be part of it. They would read about it in the papers, but more importantly, they'd see countless stories

*about the counterculture on TV. Mass communications led to
mass insecurities.*

*Madison Avenue had become obsessed with the youth
culture. The major ad agencies all began hammering at the
absurdities of our society. Suddenly the countercultural
revolution was a two-front war, fought both in the streets and
on TV. The battle against conformity had been joined.
Marlon Brando's exclamation from* The Wild Bunch, *when
he answered the question of a grown-up who asked, "What
are you rebelling against?" with "Whadda ya got?" became
our generation's mantra. This was okay with the adults as
long as it was directed toward lifestyles and not politics. In
polite society, one does not discuss religion, sex, or politics.
Since we'd completely destroyed the prevailing ethos of the
first two categories, there was justifiable concern among
adults that we'd triumph in the political arena as well.
Messing with the status quo was acceptable as long as it
confined itself to music, clothes, mating, and other social
rituals. Up until now we were just an amusing sideshow.
When we started going after their political power—no way,
this is where they drew the line.*

*At the same time, there was another component to the social
equation: the influence of the good doctor, Benjamin Spock.*

Spock's The Common Sense Book of Baby and Child Care
had a profound and lasting effect on our generation. The

book was a huge hit, outsold in the Western world only by the Bible and Shakespeare. The doctor's reassuring message to our parents—that they should trust themselves as they attended to their children's physical and psychological needs—had enormous appeal to the mothers of millions of baby boomers.

In sharp contrast to earlier child-rearing practices that called for harsh, often physical, discipline of the child, Spock advocated a permissiveness that was aimed toward providing a more pleasurable domestic life. The concept of child-centeredness fit the temperament of the time. Spock literally changed the way America raised its children.

The downside was the creation of a generation of spoiled brats.

See, there was a mighty flaw in Spock's methodology: It was driven by mothers' guilt, and—big surprise—almost all of us figured this out and feasted on our mothers' uncertainty. Our mothers, preoccupied by our every belch and bowel movement, desperately wanted to raise us correctly. So they followed Spock, and Spock told them let us be, let us do our own thing . . . and we did. It was only a matter of time until this formula of permissive behavior led to trouble. Again, everything was okay as long as all we only asked for was an alternative lifestyle, but when we wanted to change the world . . . look out.

"We want the world and we want it now," screamed Jim Morrison, and he meant it. Why not? We'd gotten everything else we'd ever wanted. Okay, now we wanted the Vietnam War to end . . . so do it!

Chicago thus became the logical conclusion to the Spock revolution. We all showed up, demanding our way, and the grown-ups, who probably suspected that they should have been tougher, put their foot down. Actually, they stomped it down on our necks, backs, and faces. Rather than sending us to our rooms, they sent us to jails and hospitals. They were going to teach us a lesson—and they did, but not the right one. Instead of learning to obey them, we learned to defy and detest them.

CHICAGO

AUGUST 1968

If you're going to Chicago,
be sure to wear some armor in your hair . . .
TODD GITLIN

The city of Chicago is one of the few major municipalities that has, at great public expense, erected a statue to its policemen. That should have been a tip-off. I mean, this was a city that obviously took its law enforcement seriously, and Chicago's cops were seriously out in force.

It was August 25, the week of the Democratic national convention, and Chicago's mayor, the honorable Richard Daley, had put eleven thousand policemen on twelve-hour shifts, called up five thousand members of the Illinois National Guard, and, just to be safe, had seventy-five hundred men from the crack 101st Airborne, equipped with flamethrowers, bazookas, and bayonets, stationed in the nearby suburbs. Finally, for good measure, over a thousand intelligence agents from the FBI, CIA, army, and navy had come to Chicago and gone undercover. Daley was not a man who was going to err on the side of caution.

I hadn't gone to Chicago as a demonstrator. I went as a journalist. Derek's father had gotten press credentials for his son and I to cover the Chicago convention. I was quite sure that this was going to be one of the most interesting weeks of my life.

That Mayor Daley would have taken the kids' threat to his city seriously is a tribute to the creativity and great drugs of Abbie

99

Hoffman and Jerry Rubin. The two of them had founded the Youth International Party or Yippies. It wasn't much of a party. Actually, that's all it was—a great party for Abbie and Jerry.

The two radical activists and self-styled revolutionary leaders were actually just a couple of clever, nice Jewish boys. Abbie, the more flamboyant of the two, was a master of the political prank. A graduate of Brandeis, with a master's degree in psychology, Abbie moved like quicksilver through the civil rights movement into radical politics. A genius in creating the "happening," Abbie was at his best when the cameras were rolling. Whether it be tossing dollar bills from the visitors' gallery onto the floor of the New York Stock Exchange, trying to levitate the Pentagon with his mental energy, or sending several thousand marijuana joints to people selected at random from the New York telephone book, Abbie always found ways to be amusing and newsworthy.

Jerry too felt that political change came from the tube of a television set. Raised in a traditional Midwestern setting, he came to Berkeley, was radicalized, and began creating "guerrilla theater" in order to foment social change. Jerry loved costume drama. He dressed in American flag diapers, judicial robes, and whatever else he could think of to mock the establishment.

Abbie and Jerry were full-time agitators. They loved being the center of attention. They loved being thought of as spokespersons of our generation. They both knew they were egomaniacs, but thought that was a good quality for a revolutionary leader. They were, as my grandmother used to say, "a couple of characters."

The boys had convinced Mayor Daley that Chicago was going to be inundated by a million stoned freaks who would force the Democratic party to conduct its business under armed guard. Abbie and Jerry realized that the media were junkies who desperately needed a fix to keep the morning newspapers and evening news interesting. They were happy to oblige. Their idea for a massive demonstration in Chicago would be called the "Festival of Life" to counterpoint the Democrats' "Politics of Death." Every day they'd leak another outlandish spectacle that they claimed would be performed at their jamboree. For example:

- A joint-rolling contest would be conducted
- Workshops on drugs, draft dodging, and guerrilla theater would be given
- A nude grope-in for peace and prosperity would take place
- All the top rock and roll acts would perform
- All the hippest poets would read
- LSD would be put into Chicago's water supply
- Yippie girls would work as hookers and slip acid into delegates' drinks
- Yippie studs would seduce delegates' wives and daughters
- A Miss Yippie contest would be held

They issued a manifesto that read: "We are dirty, smelly, grimy, foul, loud, dope-crazed, hell-bent and leather-jacketed. We are a public display of filth and shabbiness, living in-the-flesh rejects of middle-class standards. We will piss and shit and fuck in public . . . We will be constantly stoned or tripping on every drug known to man . . . Dig it! The future of humanity is in our hands!"

Finally, they announced that they would nominate their own presidential candidate—a pig aptly named Pegasus. Pegasus's platform was rather unique: he would be eaten after he won the election. This, the Yippies said, would reverse the normal process in which "the pig is elected and proceeds to eat the people."

One can only imagine Mayor Daley's state of mind as night after night he watched the media-crazed Yippies on TV. The boys knew they had to get wilder and crazier to get airtime, so they just kept turning up the decibel level:

"We will burn Chicago to the ground!" We will fuck on the beaches!" "Acid for all!" "We demand the Politics of Ecstasy!" and my personal favorite, "Abandon the Creeping Meatball!"

Of course it was all hype. Nobody wanted to bother with doing the grassroots organizing necessary to actually get kids there. It was way more fun to be on television than to stuff envelopes.

Poor Daley and his minions took the Yippies seriously. He turned Chicago into an armed camp. He made it very clear to the youth of America: Come to Chicago and take your chances. We're ready for you.

The intimidation worked. Instead of a million kids, about five or six thousand showed up. It's just as well, because the Festival of Life quickly turned into a police riot.

Derek and I checked into our hotel. A postage-stamp-sized decal of Mayor Daley was stuck onto the phone: "Welcome to Chicago." We decided to wander over to Lincoln Park. This was the nerve center for the Festival.

My first impression was that of being in a theater. Everyone seemed to be trying to put on some kind of show. People were dancing, chanting, and arguing, and a few of the more uninhibited ones displayed affection like late-night cable television porn stars. I wandered over to a large group standing around Jerry Rubin. He had his candidate Pegasus with him on a leash.

Jerry was about to take his hog downtown to the Picasso sculpture, known in Chicago as the gooney bird, and hold a press conference. He was going to demand Secret Service protection for his candidate and wanted a foreign policy briefing for the pig. (Pegasus was later arrested and escaped the convention unharmed.)

Abbie Hoffman, not to be outdone, was showing people a copy of the *Chicago Tribune*. The fact that anyone took him seriously continued to amaze Abbie, but if they wanted to play, he'd make the game interesting. A couple of days before, meeting with city negotiators to try and get permits for a march, he'd told them, with a straight face, that he'd call the whole thing off and leave town for a hundred thousand dollars in American greenbacks. The *Tribune* headline screamed: YIPPIES DEMAND CASH FROM CITY!

Abbie was telling a small group of his latest idea. He wanted to collect as many draft cards as he could and burn them en masse in front of the convention amphitheater, spelling out BEAT ARMY.

A very pretty girl with the unlikely name of Plum was hanging with Abbie. Well, he was a star. She was passing out handbills. You can imagine what any sane adult, let alone one as tense and paranoid as Mayor Daley, must have felt on reading the text.

YIPPIE

Lincoln Park

VOTE PIG IN 68

Free Motel

"come sleep with us"

REVOLUTION TOWARDS A FREE
SOCIETY: YIPPIE!

By A. Yippie

1. An immediate end to the War in Vietnam

2. Immediate freedom for Huey Newton

3. The legalization of marijuana and all other psychedelic drugs

4. Total disarmament of all the people beginning with the police

5. The abolition of money

6. The elimination of pollution

7. Student power to determine his or her course of study

8. The end of all censorship

9. We believe that people should fuck all the time, anytime, with whomever they wish

Political Pigs, your days are numbered. We are the Second American Revolution. We shall win. Yippie!

Hey, if that wasn't a platform you can get behind, what was?

I asked the girl how exactly she envisioned a society devoid of money might work. She gave me a warm, gentle smile. "People would just do their own thing."

"Whose thing would it be to collect the garbage?" I asked.

Abbie came over to join us.

"Why are you trying to bum trip Plum?"

"I'm not," I answered. "I just have a couple of questions about your manifesto." I was trying to act like a journalist; thus I was wearing my press credential. (Actually I was just trying to show off.) Abbie saw I was press and for the next few minutes he was mine.

"How is a world without money going to function?" I asked him.

"Well, for one thing, you won't have to worry about pay toilets," Abbie beamed. Plum laughed adoringly. One thing about Abbie, he was fast and funny.

"But who would want to do the mundane chores of . . ." I tried to continue.

"Let the machines do it, man," he said. "Couldn't you dig a society in which people are free from the drudgery of work?"

"Sure, but . . ." I stammered. I wasn't used to going up against such an agile, absurd mind.

"Think about it, man. No pay housing for the people, free transportation, free food, free education and clothing and medical. You got a problem with that?"

I didn't want to debate the guy. What I really wanted to do was discuss with Plum the plank in the Yippie program about people making love all the time, anytime, with whomever they wished, but Abbie was relentless.

"C'mon, let's hear some more of your liberal bullshit," he pressed.

"It's just absurd. Who's going to work if everything is free?"

"BINGO!" Abbie began jumping up and down. "That's what we want! A society that strives toward and actively promotes the concept of full unemployment. How can you not dig that?" Plum put her arm around Abbie and cuddled up to him.

"That's the stupidest thing I've ever heard," I sputtered.

Abbie pulled Plum closer. He jabbed me in the chest with his finger.

"Listen, guy, you're either part of the problem or part of the solution. Why don't you go back to your 'clean for Gene' friends and let us get on with the revolution?"

What could I say? I left the park and went across the street to the Hilton to check out the McCarthy Magical Mystery Tour.

Eugene McCarthy, the Democratic senator from Minnesota, had put the fear of God into the Democratic party. Running as an anti-Vietnam War candidate, he'd become a rallying point for both young and old who wanted to send a message to President Johnson. McCarthy was an acid-tongued, Catholic intellectual; his incredibly strong showing in the New Hampshire and Wisconsin primaries had broken both LBJ's heart and spirit. The president declared "*no más*" and quit the fight.

With Johnson out, his vice president Hubert Humphrey and New York Democratic senator Robert Kennedy were in. Humphrey had the party apparatus behind him, but not much support from the general population. McCarthy and Kennedy ran against each other in a series of cantankerous primary battles, culminating with

Kennedy's victory in the California primary. Shortly after his acceptance speech Robert Kennedy was assassinated.

Coming on the heels of Martin Luther King's brutal assassination just a couple of months earlier, Kennedy's death left the Democratic Party in a moral vacuum. Politicos, like nature, abhor this, and within a short time Democratic Party regulars had sewn up the requisite number of delegates Humphrey needed for the nomination.

McCarthy, being a guy who'd rather discuss Gaelic poetry with smart, attractive women than stump for votes, withdrew into himself and lost his fighting edge. His followers, however, especially the younger ones, still hoped that the convention would reignite their man. They had worked long, hard hours for many months and desperately wanted some kind of payoff, and, being baby boomers, they couldn't imagine that they wouldn't get what they wanted.

The McCarthy kids were bright, clean-cut, overachievers. I stood in the doorway of their suite at the Hilton watching them. They were all scurrying around doing as much busy work as they could find. The kids across the street had no problem just hanging in the park, lying in the grass, getting high, rapping on the new world order. These kids were their polar opposites. Manic in their enthusiasm, they had to be working toward some goal, even if it was just producing a meaningless pamphlet to slide under delegates' doors that night.

Unlike the kids across the street, these kids did not believe that we had to force a confrontation with the authorities to reveal the true nature of the beast that was America. They liked the United States. It just needed some fine-tuning.

One of them quoted Anne Frank. Like Frank, she believed that "in spite of everything people are really good at heart." Another kid told me he didn't want to burn the flag—just wash it.

I spent a couple of hours talking with them. They were really boring. It was much more fun in the park. I hurried back over to see how the street people's "Abandon the Creeping Meatball" campaign was progressing.

The real action was now taking place at Grant Park, about a quarter mile east of the Hilton. I wandered down to the band shell where the Mobilization, a militant anti-everything political party, was holding a rally. There was a fairly good-sized crowd already there, probably close to six or seven thousand kids. People were sitting around listening to big-shot radicals scream down at them from a bullhorn on the bandstand. Three sides of the bandstand were surrounded by Chicago's finest. They did not look like they were in a very good mood.

During this past week they'd had to work long, frustrating hours. Tired of the kids screaming "Kill the pigs" and "Your wife sucks cock" at them, and susceptible to their Mayor's contagious paranoia, the police of Chicago were getting to really dislike the kids. There was also a class issue. Most of the cops were second-generation Americans whose parents had struggled to make it to the middle class. They had been fiercely disciplined at home— most of their mothers hadn't used Dr. Spock's book to raise them. They viewed the demonstrators as spoiled little rich kids who needed to learn a lesson.

While the speeches continued, a couple of street kids climbed a flag pole next to the bandstand and cut down the American flag. They started to put up a red Vietcong banner or something. That did it. The cops had had enough. A squad of them charged the pole, dragged down the youthful offenders and began whopping them. This was not such a good idea, since the police squad quickly became surrounded by the kids, who began pelting the cops with rocks and bottles. The police fired tear gas canisters, but the wind shifted and the gas came right back at the cops. The squad of policemen began to panic and brutally fought their way free of the crowd.

I stood there watching, amazed. This was so much better than television—and it was live. And the kids had won! Or so it seemed.

Rennie Davis, one of the Mobilization leaders, took the bullhorn and began yelling at us to all stay calm and sit down. He was midsentence when a much larger force of police charged. Two cops came up behind Rennie and—WHOMP!—let him have it with their clubs. He fell unconscious, a huge cut on the back of his head. I stood there horrified. I'd seen fights in my high school but I'd never seen anybody hit like that. This was getting very real.

Tom Hayden, another movement leader and Jane Fonda's future husband, grabbed the bullhorn. Rennie was a good friend of his and he was just short of hysterical.

"The city and the military machinery it has aimed at us won't permit us to protest in an organized fashion," Tom screamed. He pointed to the edge of the park. "Therefore, we must move out of this park in groups throughout the city, and turn this overheated military machine against itself. Let us make sure that if blood flows, it flows all over the city."

I'd heard enough, especially about the blood flowing stuff. It was definitely time to leave the park.

The problem was that getting out of Grant Park was not so easy. It's not really a park. It's actually a series of strips of greenery cut between the main street, Michigan Avenue, and Lake Michigan. To get back into the city we had to cross bridges. There were a number of bridges we could cross, but the police had blocked almost all of them. We were trapped in the park.

More and more police arrived on the scene. Then the National Guard showed up. Dressed in their khaki green military outfits with cool tin-cup helmets, and carrying rifles, they looked like real soldiers rather than the fellow draft-dodging kids that they actually were.

A group of kids tried to rush one of the bridges, attempting to break free into the city. They were repulsed by a barrage of tear gas. We were trapped. I took my press credential out of my pocket and pinned it onto my shirt.

I moved away from the heavily guarded bridges and headed north. Each bridge across from Grant was guarded by police and National Guardsmen. I began to jog. I ran for about a quarter mile. Each bridge along the way was blocked. Finally I got lucky. One of the bridges had only a handful of cops guarding it. A group of kids charged and the cops withdrew. We had an exit point! I joined a stampede of kids who scampered across the bridge to Michigan Avenue. I was in the Loop. I looked around, trying to get my bearings. It was between six and seven in the evening, still light out. It's not often in life you get to do a true double take, but I did one as I saw, coming slowly down Michigan Avenue, three mule-drawn wagons. I walked over and took a closer look.

It was the Reverend Ralph Abernathy and his Poor Peoples' Campaign. Abernathy was a close friend of the late Martin Luther King and his successor as head of the Southern Christian Leadership Conference. Earlier that year, he had led a large contingent of blacks into Washington, DC to erect what they called Resurrection City, U.S.A. in the mall between the Lincoln Memorial and the Washington Monument. Thousands had come there to live in tents and, like the Bonus marchers of the 1930s, draw attention to the economic conditions from which so many of their brothers and sisters suffered. It was meant as a protest against poverty and they hoped to arouse the conscience of the nation.

Now the wagon train was in Chicago to again try to raise the conscience of the nation to the cause. The city, I guess afraid of pissing off the predominantly African-American South Side, gave the Reverend Abernathy a permit to march his wagons to the convention hall. I quickly joined an impromptu group of street people and fell into step behind the mules. More and more people were able to escape from the park. Most of them joined us. People along Michigan Avenue also began to join in. Soon there were a few thousand of us marching behind the wagons.

That evening's twilight in Chicago had a surreal quality to it. The streets reeked of tear gas. All of us—eyes red and stinging, exhilarated that we'd broken out of the park, furious at the police, overtired, scared, and high on each other's energy—marched gallantly down Michigan Avenue toward the Hilton. If we could just get to the amphitheater, four miles away, we could let the delegates know how deeply we felt about the war, we could . . .

At Balboa Avenue, a block away from the Hilton, everyone stopped. The police had formed a barricade across the sidewalk to prevent us from going any further. I still felt safe. It was the mules. I didn't think the police would attack helpless mules. We stood there waiting. Nobody seemed to be in charge.

To the right of us I noticed large number of policemen beginning to take up their positions. I walked back a block and looked down the next street. It too was blocked by police. I started to walk across the street to the park, but the bridges were still blocked by the police. I looked down toward the end of the march. A number of police cars were arriving and men were jumping out and taking up positions. We were surrounded.

I walked back toward the front of the march. The mules were gone! The Poor People's march had been allowed to cross Balboa Avenue, but no demonstrators.

A red-headed guy with a beard began wrapping a bandanna around his mouth and putting Vaseline on his cheeks (for tear gas). He looked over at me and smiled.

"Gonna get very heavy here," he said. He pointed at my press pass. "Take that off if I was you. First people the cops are gonna want to take out are newsies."

I took the pass off and put it in my pocket.

Up ahead was the Hilton and right across the street from it was my hotel. If I could get to my hotel before . . .

Too late.

A fuselage of tear gas canisters rained down on us. Suddenly everyone was screaming.

The police charged us. "Shit," the redhead next to me said. "They took off their badges." They'd figured if they couldn't be identified they could do whatever they wanted. They were right.

I decided to stay with my original strategy and ran toward my hotel. The police were everywhere, cutting through the crowd and smashing anyone they could catch. I saw a number of people clubbed down from behind. Once down, the victims were set upon like animals felled by a pack of wolves. Clubs beat onto skulls with sickening thuds. I had never been so scared in my life.

Somehow I dodged my way through the mayhem and made it to the front of my hotel. Two policemen and a number of hotel security guards stood at the front entrance. I tried to make my way in. One of the cops grabbed me.

"I'm staying here!" I yelled.

He ignored me and took out his nightstick. I pulled free of him and ripped my shirt. He swung and missed. I took off. The policeman began to chase me, but other kids were heading for the door so he returned to his post.

I ran across the street to the Hilton. Suddenly I heard a loud crash. The window to the Haymarket Inn, a restaurant in the Hilton facing Michigan Avenue, had been shattered by the weight of spectators who had been crushing against it from the street side.

I ran around the corner and jumped through the window.

Inside the restaurant all hell had broken loose. Police had charged into the room and were clubbing anyone they could get their hands on, including those who, moments earlier, had been peacefully drinking in the hotel bar. I remember noticing a sign as I ran through: *The Haymarket Lounge—A place where good guys take good girls to dine in the lusty, rollicking atmosphere of fabulous Old Chicago.* It was rollicking, all right. Waitresses wearing tiny Gay Nineties dresses with miniskirts and deep décolletages were screaming bloody murder. The place smelled of tear gas, fear, and stink bombs that the Yippies had set off a couple of days before. If Dante had wanted to create a modern ring of Hell, this would have passed.

I made it out of the restaurant and into the lobby and I ran for a bank of elevators; miraculously a car appeared. I jumped in and pushed the button for the top floor.

When I got off the elevator it was strangely quiet. At the end of the hall a door was open. I walked in and found myself in *Newsweek* magazine's hospitality suite. A number of reporters were looking down on the street below, where the riot continued. I joined them and watched with both fascination and horror while the police beat on the kids down below.

Finally one of the *Newsweek* guys noticed me. He looked at my torn shirt and asked me if I'd been in the street. I nodded and he took out a notebook and began interviewing me. It was weird.

"Do you think the police are overreacting?" he asked.

We looked down at the park and watched a doctor in a white uniform and Red Cross armband run toward a kid sitting with rivulets of blood running down his long blond hair. Two cops caught the doctor from behind and knocked him down. One began clubbing the man's rib cage.

"Are you out of your GODDAMN mind!" I screamed at the poor reporter. "Why don't you go down there and do something!"

"Look, kid, I don't make the news. I just report it. Personally I think this is . . ." We watched as the doctor tried to get away from the cops and they followed him, bashing him with their nightsticks.

"Oh, fuck it!" The guy said, obviously as sickened as I was. "Why did you kids come here anyway?"

I thought for a beat and turned to go. "Because you're either part of the problem or part of the solution."

CULVER CITY

SEPTEMBER 1968

*The urge to violence rises in proportion
to the frustration of peaceful change . . .*
KINGMAN BREWSTER, PRESIDENT, YALE UNIVERSITY

When I got home there was still no word from Yu Lin. Her parents must have locked her up or something. I had no idea if any of my letters had reached her.

I did have two other letters waiting for me. One was from Yale University informing me that Kenneth Scott Latourette had been tragically killed crossing the street that summer in Portland, Oregon and obviously would no longer be available for me to study with. The other was from the University of California, Berkeley, telling me that I'd been accepted into their East Asian studies graduate school.

In the background, Mayor Daley was holding his first press conference since the convention. I was sad that I couldn't work with Dr. Latourette. He was a great man and a seminal figure in the study of Chinese affairs. It was another of life's strange what ifs.

I had just had Yu Lin yanked out of my life by the police and been chased and almost beaten by them as well in Chicago. What better place to get in touch with my feelings about authority figures than Berkeley?

I watched Mayor Daley stare intently back at me on our TV. Earlier they'd shown a rerun of him waving his fist at Senator Abraham Ribicoff of Connecticut, who had stood at the Democratic convention podium denouncing the "gestapo tactics of Mayor Daley's police." Daley had yelled back, "Fuck you, you Jew son of a bitch, you lousy motherfuckers go home."

Now Daley again spoke to America.

"Let's get this thing straight once and for all. The police aren't there to create disorder; the policeman is there to preserve disorder."

Berkeley

Dissent and doubt versus law and order. Sit-ins and student strikes against police and National Guard occupation of campuses. Institutions of higher learning had become microcosms for the drama that was playing out in our land. In early 1968 President Johnson eradicated all draft deferments for graduate students. Suddenly baby boomers were faced with the prospect of having to go and fight in a war they detested. There was something terribly wrong with America.

It had already been a cataclysmic year. The assassinations of Martin Luther King and Robert Kennedy had shocked and sickened the country. The Tet Offensive in Vietnam had shown how far away we were from a meaningful resolution of the war. President Johnson, battered and confused by his people's lack of support and enthusiasm for the conflict, decided to pack it in and not seek reelection, and headed back to his ranch. Riots in our cities and campuses shook the nation and intensified mistrust between the races and the generations. America seemed on the brink of imploding.

On the best-seller list that year was Eldridge Cleaver's Soul on Ice, *but the Black Panther leader wasn't going out on an author's tour: He'd fled to Cuba to avoid going to prison for parole violations. Other significant titles were* Armies of the Night *by Norman Mailer, recounting his experiences during the anti-war demonstrations the year before in Washington, and* The Algiers Motel Incident *by John Hersey, an account of the murder of three blacks by police during riots in Detroit. The Pulitzer Prize went to William Styron for* The Confessions of Nat Turner, *the story of a slave uprising. None of them exactly light reading, these popular books reflected the supercharged atmosphere that gripped the country.*

In music, things were equally intense. "John Wesley Harding" by Bob Dylan, "Jumping Jack Flash" by the Rolling Stones, and "Hey Jude" by the Beatles were enormous hits, while Led Zeppelin No. 1 *and* Cheap Thrills *were huge sellers. On television,* Rowan and Martin's Laugh-In, Gunsmoke, Hawaii Five-O, Mayberry R.F.D, *and a new show called* 60 Minutes *were the hits.* Rosemary's Baby, 2001, Planet of the Apes, *and* Night of the Living Dead *were among the top grossing films of the year.*

———

One of the most striking things about the student upheavals taking place in the late 60s was how universal they seemed to be. National boundaries didn't matter. It was kids versus grown-ups worldwide. England, Japan, Poland, Germany, Italy, Hungary, Sweden, Yugoslavia, Belgium, Czechoslovakia, Spain, and France all had major student activist movements. World communications let us hear about what the kids in other countries were doing and made us feel like we were part of a world community. We also knew that we were the eye of the storm. Kids in Prague watched as we protested. Kids at the Sorbonne wanted to know what was happening on our campuses. Our demonstrations were not only staged for domestic consumption, but, as we had chanted to mayor Daley in Chicago, "The whole world is watching."

The political militancy we felt was pervasive. A Gallup poll that year found that eighty-one percent of undergraduates were dissatisfied with their schools. Nearly five hundred universities had strikes or were forced to shut down. We knew we had momentum and that we were going to stomp the reactionary warmongers right out of power.

Of course we might have exaggerated our own sense of power. In fact, the hostile reaction to our behavior was quickly beginning to boil to the surface. Our newly elected vice president, the esteemed Spiro T. Agnew, said our universities were "circus tents or psychiatric centers for overprivileged, underdisciplined, irresponsible children of well-to-do blasé permissivists." Okay. In fact, parents and most other adults were, as Oregon's governor Tom McCall said, "fed up to their eardrums and eyeballs" with us.

We assumed they were jealous. "Don't trust anyone over thirty!" was our maxim. If they were so down on us, why were they imitating us? They seemed obsessed with the youth culture. For the first time kids were setting fashion for adults. Plastic surgeons made a fortune trying to bring youth back to grown-ups. The currency of the age was no longer money—it was youth. We were the Now Generation.

Through most of our history, whenever grown-ups felt they had a problem with their kids, the laboratory they turned to for solutions was the school. If radical and subversive behavior was the problem, education must have the answer. They figured everything could be worked out on campus with the proper instruction. Boy, were they in for a surprise.

BERKELEY

We are not flowers in a greenhouse;
we are pine trees in the storm . . .
MAO-TSE DYLAN

I would venture to say that being a graduate student at Berkeley in 1968/1969 was the most fun time to be alive in the history of the world.

Why:

You could sleep with anyone

You could eat anything

You could take any drug

You could say anything

You could live off the fat of the land

You could feel you were going to change the world

You could be as outrageous as you wanted

Why Not:

None of it would last

My first day in Berkeley. I was walking down Telegraph Avenue, the main drag in front of the university. The shops were about what you'd expect in a college town, but the people? I'd never seen anything like it. I was at the epicenter of the hippie world. The clothes were amazing. It was an explosion of colors, tie-dyed shirts, granny dresses, granny glasses, and everyone was letting their "freak flag" fly. Hair everywhere.

A black guy came up to me and opened a small box. Inside was a virtual drugstore of psychedelics, acid, marijuana, speed, psilocybin, the works. He described his wares, sounding like an encyclopedia salesman.

A kid stumbled over and bought a hit of acid from the guy. He started to walk away, then came back and grabbed my arm. He looked intently into my eyes and passed on these words of wisdom:

"LSD is like Ban deodorant. Ban takes the worry out of being close; LSD takes the worry out of being." Then he stumbled off into the crowd. This was going to be some year.

Two years before I arrived in Berkeley I was named *Time* magazine's Man of the Year. Actually, it wasn't just me. It was the entire under-twenty-five generation. "Today's young people are the most intensely discussed and dissected generation in history," *Time* said, then went on to gush, "With his skeptical yet humanistic outlook, his disdain for fanaticism and his scorn for the spurious, the Man of the Year suggests that he will infuse the future with a new sense of morality, a transcendent and contemporary ethic that could infinitely enrich the 'empty society.' If he succeeds the Man of the Year will be a man indeed—and have a great deal of fun in the process."

Well, okay, I guess they could have been a bit more off. They could have predicted that we'd all go live in caves. As I looked around the street, however, all I saw was rampant fanaticism and total admiration for the spurious.

The zeitgeist of Berkeley in the late 60s was "Let it be now!" As reported, we had rejected *cogito, ergo sum* and replaced it with *sum, ergo sum.*

As I walked into my new home, a small apartment house on the south side of campus, I passed under a banner nailed up over our front door. It read:

IF IT FEELS GOOD, DO IT!

My first night at school I went out with my new roommates looking for bananas. One of the guys in the house had assured us that the insides of banana peels produced a legal, marijuana-like high. We raced to a nearby market, but every banana in the store had been sold!

We rushed to another store—banana-less. Now we were getting desperate. We split up and agreed to meet back at the house with our fruit. I didn't know my way around Berkeley and didn't have a car, so I gave up after a half hour and went back to the house and waited. An hour later one of our housemates came back with some bananas. He'd driven all the way to San Francisco for them. There was not a banana to be had in the entire city of Berkeley.

Of course, you can't actually get high on banana peels; the whole thing had been a hoax. But the point was that the whole community had believed it and was willing to try it. Hundreds, probably thousands of kids had rampaged through the city that night, grabbing up bananas on the off chance that they'd get a low-cost high. That's what made Berkeley so fascinating. The whole place was nuts.

Despite all, I became a serious student. My first two semesters at Cal I carried a perfect 4.0 grade point average. None of my teachers from Culver would have believed it.

I majored in East Asian studies and had some fantastic professors. It was a case of the more I learned, the more I wanted to know. Chinese history fascinated me. Due to my years in Taiwan, my language skills were far ahead of those of most of the other students in the department. Thus, I wasn't saddled with learning Chinese, and I could take virtually any classes I wished.

In addition to my classwork, I was also running Dispatch News Service, an anti-war news service devoted to telling the "truth" about what was happening in Vietnam.

One of the true bastions of sanity I was able to locate while living in Taipei was a coffeehouse called the Yeh Run (the Barbarian). There various expatriates would hang with what passed for China's avant garde, and over cigarettes and bootleg jazz we'd discuss man's fate. (Both the book and the circumstances.)

It was at the Yeh Run that I was first able to share with my friends some of the horrible stories I'd been hearing from the GIs I'd met in the bars. Their descriptions of what was going on in Nam were nothing like what I'd been reading in the newspapers. Tales of rifles not working in the jungle, equipment being stolen by our South Vietnamese allies, inept officers and corrupt officials, were told by all. What was most unsettling was the almost casual way they described the killing. The killing of "gooks."

My other friends in Taiwan had heard equally grim stories. But why didn't the rest of the country know about it? We were convinced that the journalists in Vietnam were either incredibly lazy or being lied to. We wanted people to know the truth. It was simple. We would form Dispatch News Service and tell people the facts. We thought that if Americans really knew what was going down in Vietnam, the war would be over in a minute. We were very young.

It was my job to get Dispatch's stories into American newspapers. Once a week I would receive copy from Saigon. I would mimeograph the stories, type them up on the Dispatch stationary my father designed for us, stuff them into envelopes, and send them out to newspapers. I began calling on editors in the Bay Area. All I asked was that they read our stuff. Amazingly enough, they did. Dispatch copy began to run in the *National Catholic Reporter,* the *San Francisco Chronicle,* and other mainstream papers. The *Seattle Times* began running Dispatch. I got the *Daily Cal* and the UCLA student paper, the *Daily Bruin,* to begin running our stuff. I went to a couple of student conferences and got a bunch of editors from other college papers to run it as well. We were getting the word out and it was the best high I'd ever known. There would be our story, complete with the Dispatch byline, for hundreds of thousands of people to see. This was big stuff.

BERKELEY

Youth have bad manners,
contempt for authority, disrespect for their elders.
Children nowadays are tyrants . . .
SOCRATES

It was about this time that I met Orville Schell. Orville, also a graduate student in Chinese, was unique for two special reasons. The first was that he'd already co-published, along with Berkeley professor Franz Schurmann, a three-volume *China Reader,* which had become one of the standard texts for our department. The second was that he was the first person I'd ever heard use the term *groovy.*

Orville was also opposed to the Vietnam War, and he and a number of others had formed a group called the Committee of Concerned Asian Scholars (CCAS). Orville asked me to join. I was thrilled for a number of reasons. To begin with, it was the first group I'd belonged to since the Boy Scouts of America. (I wasn't a big joiner in high school, although in my senior yearbook I listed myself as belonging to the nonexistent Folk Music Club.) Second, like the others in our group, I was intensely concerned about Asians and what American troops were doing to them. Last, I loved the idea of being in a group of people that called themselves scholars.

Our meetings consisted of a lot of intense discussion about what should be done to end the war, arguments about tactics, and maneuverings for positions of power within the group. What we really did was take a lot of votes. We voted on everything from our official name to the color of our stationary.

One of our members, Alfred, was far more radical than the rest of us. He couldn't stand our prolonged discussions. "Talk, talk, talk—aren't we ever going to *do* anything?" he demanded.

"Like what?" asked Orville.

"Like go up to Seattle and trash the Association of Asian Studies Convention." Alfred replied. We all looked at each other for a beat and quickly voted—Yes! A ROAD TRIP!

This was before the movie *Animal House.* We didn't know about bringing togas and kegs of beer with us, but our general plan was similar to that of John Belushi and the boys. We'd jump in the car, hit the road, and have a ball—oh, and on the way, try to end the Vietnam War. It took us two days to drive up from Berkeley to Seattle. Along the way we continued to vote on various issues. Should we participate in the discussions at the conference or just disrupt them? We voted to wait until we saw what was going on before deciding.

When we got there we stayed with the brother of one of the CCAS guys in his frat house (please, always refer to it as a fraternity, he patiently told us). We crashed on couches and the floor and had a fabulous time. The night we arrived the house was having a mixer with a sorority. We voted unanimously that we should attend the party and try to raise the women's political consciousness.

Alfred, much more focused than the rest of us, somehow got us up the next morning and over to the University of Washington campus where the Association of Asian Studies was having its annual national conference. Various workshops and lectures on topics ranging from Sung dynasty scroll painting to the dynamics of Japan's economic success were given by the most preeminent professors and scholars in American academia. We were only interested in one of the seminars, "American Foreign Policy and

Vietnam." The meeting was being held in a classroom on the university campus.

The Association of Asian Studies is the most prestigious body in the field of Oriental studies. To be asked to speak at its conference is recognition of a professor's standing in his or her discipline and is considered a great honor. It is a reward for years of hard work in the professor's field. Those professors who tried to lecture at the seminar we attended probably didn't feel it was such a wonderful payoff.

We marched into the room and stood behind a couple of tables at which about a dozen professors were seated. One of the men, the chairman, motioned for us to move to the back of the room where folding chairs had been placed for the audience.

Alfred leaned forward and softly spoke to the man, "We suggest you change your theme." The specific topic that the learned men were to speak on that morning was "Vietnam: Patterns of Growth in a Maturing Political Process."

"We think the issue to discuss should be 'Vietnam: Patterns of American Genocide,' " Alfred boomed.

The chairman looked up at Alfred and the rest of us in horror. He got to his feet. "How dare you come in here and disrupt this . . ."

"How dare you not discuss the pointless slaughter of innocent men, women, and children in a senseless war," Alfred roared back.

Another graying eminence stood up. He pointed at us and said, "Don't you people have any manners?"

"What does manners have to do with this?" Alfred answered. "Manners? Christ, if the Vietcong knew which soup spoon to use, would you stop bombing them?"

The older man stood with his finger shaking. "You are no gentleman."

Time for me to put in my two cents worth. I walked over to him.

"Gentleman? You think that you and your government are gentlemen? First of all, what kind of man drops hundreds of thousands of tons of napalm on people? Certainly not one that's gentle."

Another professorial type jumped to his feet, "Get these boys' names!"

Orville tried to reason with them. "Listen, all we're asking is that you turn this meeting into a forum where we can discuss our views on the tragedy of what's taking place in Vietnam."

The professorial type turned bright red. "If by some miracle you're ever given tenure and become a full professor, then you can dictate what's discussed at these meetings. Until then, sit down and be quiet!" (Ironically, Orville is now dean of the University of California's School of Communications.)

I stepped up to the professor and put my face next to his. "No! We're not going to be quiet. Thousands of people will die in Vietnam just while you're having this conference. We're not going to . . ."

My sermon was suddenly interrupted by a loud crash. Alfred had overturned one of their tables. He walked to the next one and neatly flipped it over as well. Papers, notebooks, and water glasses crashed to the floor.

"Call the police!" yelled the chairman. One of the professors ran out the door.

We quickly huddled.

"What did you do that for?" I asked Alfred.

"It's all bullshit. We needed to show these motherfuckers we mean business," he answered.

The head of our group took over. "Okay, we've got to decide what we're going to do. Stay or split? If we stay we'll probably be arrested."

"I'm out of here. I have a Japanese midterm on Monday," said Alfred.

"I don't think we're going to raise these guys' political consciousness by going to jail," I said. I tried to sound like the Lone Ranger. "Come on men, our work is done here." We voted to leave.

We all headed for the door. Alfred began chanting and we all joined in. "Ho, Ho, Ho Chi Min, NLF is going to win. Ho, Ho, Ho Chi Min, NLF is going to win."

We ran to the car and took off, full of revolutionary fervor, proud that we'd done our part for the struggle and had undoubtedly helped the masses of the third world. We voted to give Alfred a letter of commendation for his heroic actions. We also voted not to give our real names if asked about Alfred's same heroic actions. Finally, in a close vote, we elected to stop at McDonald's and have lunch.

BERKELEY

A little rebellion is a good thing . . .
THOMAS JEFFERSON

I began to settle into a routine. Classes in the morning, Dispatch in the afternoon, library at night. Of course I had a social life (hey, this was Berkeley in the 60s), but most of my time was spent either working on school or anti-war stuff. Around mid-February my routine was shattered.

I was sitting in my contemporary Chinese history class when I heard some guys running down the hallway shouting, "Get your asses out of classes—join the masses!"

The whole class rushed outside to see what was happening. Suddenly someone shouted, "Wheeler Auditorium is on fire." Sure enough, it was burning. Welcome to the TWLF (Third World Liberation Front) strike of 1969.

The issues of the strike were rather vague. Something about not enough black studies programs. Soon Chicanos, Asians, and Native Americans were jumping on board the strike bandwagon. They wanted more classes so they could discover their historical destinies. Oh, and incidentally, the university better make these programs student-controlled—preferably by them. Various coalitions of radical student groups banded together and presented the university with a list of demands which were, of course, rejected.

So now it was time for a student strike. Cool. We all marched to Sather Gate, which was at the top of Sproul Plaza, the central meeting place on the Cal campus. We began chanting:

"Ashes to ashes,
Dust to dust,
We hate to shut it down,
but we must we must!"

"Umph!
Umgawa!
Third World Power!"

And, of course, everyone's favorite, "Power to the People!"

I guess I felt that honoring the strike was important. You have to remember, this was a pretty strange year at Cal:

- The Golden Bears' African-American basketball players had forced both the school's athletic director and coach to resign over racial issues.

- The Cal football team had a minor race riot and a white player was found shot just outside the boys' gym.

- The school refused to let Chicano students honor Cesar Chavez's boycott against nonunion grapes.

- Ninety percent of Cal's student body was white and a lot of us felt guilty about it.

With everything in total racial disarray, it was hard not to join in when African-Americans called for racial justice. Many of us stopped going to classes in honor of the strike. Others of us, myself included, actually participated in more proactive activities to help shut the place down.

For example, we attacked the library. Big mistake. I think the idea was to capture the card catalog or something. We flew into the building, and there, arms linked, defending the catalogs, was every woman in the library science department. They looked mean and determined. We beat a hasty retreat.

Not quite so humorous was the inclusion of the Oakland Police Department's tactical squad into the equation.

Hatefully called the "blue meanies" (after the villains from the Beatles' *Yellow Submarine* movie) because of their tasteless blue jumpsuits, these guys were, tough, vicious, and in no mood to fool around.

We were all standing around Sather Gate waiting to see what the cops were going to do. It was a pretty large group of people, so I wasn't too concerned. Anyway, I'd gone through this before in Chicago. I turned to the guy next me. He was pretty clean-cut, but we had some support from "straight" kids on campus. I thought he could be a member of PL (Progressive Labor), a Maoist breakaway from the Communist Party whose members believed that you had to get disciplined and that "bourgeois tendencies such as beards and long hair turn the masses off." Anyway, I made eye contact with him and he nodded.

"We gotta end Regents' racism," I said.

"Right on," he answered.

"This kind of student solidarity is what we gotta show 'em."

"Right on."

I made a fist. "Power to the people."

"Right on," he said again.

Suddenly the blue meanies charged out of the administration building. They fired a barrage of tear gas canisters at us. All at once the guy I'd been talking to reached into his jacket and pulled out a blackjack! An undercover cop!

He looked at me and smiled. "Right on!" he yelled and charged at me. I took off as fast as I could toward the student union. He chased after me, continuing to yell, "Right on."

Luckily, in the ensuing confusion I lost the guy (in those days I would have called him a pig). I made it to the student union, ducked into the building, and watched as the blue meanies proceeded to beat the living crap out of anyone they caught. I was starting to see a pattern here.

The next day we rioted again. They brought in more cops and more meanies. Eventually they brought in the National Guard and overwhelmed us. We gave up the strike and went back to class. But this was just the prelim. The main event was about to come.

BERKELEY

If called by a panther, don't anther . . .
OGDEN NASH

The concept of adolescence was invented about the same time as the steam engine. They were both to cause Western civilization a great deal of trouble. Prior to this, you were either a child, taken care of in the home, or an adult, out in the world, contributing to the well-being of the family unit. With the advent of the industrial revolution there came about that netherworld in which children in their teens were allowed to be both childlike in their actions and grown up in their privileges. Fortunately, for both society and the adolescents, the teens grow out of it.

During a great deal of their adolescence, kids are in school. This is both the good news and the bad news. The tension between what the Germans call *lernfreiheit,* or student freedom, and our ingrained sense of giving schools the responsibility of in loco parentis has been around for a couple hundred years. The ebb and flow between strict, no-nonsense discipline and the rights of youth to question authority is a fascinating phenomenon. The extremes between a Calvinist classroom of the mid-eighteenth century and Mao Zedong's Red Guards in the mid-1960s are easy to chart and understand. It is far more difficult to find the right balance between the two poles.

At Berkeley, in the late 60s, the needle had swung off the compass.

We felt that grown-ups didn't know what was going on. We were sure that it was the rule of the ignorant over the enlightened. For example, the man who represented Berkeley in the state assembly at the time, Don Mulford, was a conservative Republican who went on record as proposing the death penalty for marijuana dealers.

Spiro Agnew (interestingly enough, an anagram of Agnew's name is GROW A PENIS!), then governor of Maryland and soon to be a heartbeat away from the presidency, led a crusade to ban the Beatles tune "With a Little Help from My Friends" because it mentioned getting high. (Here was a man who'd never taken a newspaper taxi or seen a marmalade sky.)

Conversely, the kids were driving the adults crazy. For example, our Yippie friend Jerry Rubin was meeting with the administration to try and work out the logistics for some march. He screamed at the chancellor of the University, "We can't be coopted because we want everything!" Okay, pretty good opening for a negotiation.

During the student riots at Columbia University, their poor president, Grayson Kirk, tried to sit down and reason with the demonstrators. He said, "Our young people appear to reject all forms of authority and they have taken refuge in a turbulent and inchoate nihilism whose sole objectives are destructive. I know of no time in our history when the gap between the generations has been wider or more potentially dangerous." Mark Rudd, student leader, had a pithy response: "Up against the wall, motherfucker!" Superimposed on this chasm were both the horror of the Vietnam War and the changing landscape of American racial politics.

The year before, in February, Huey Newton, a militant black leader, was stopped in Oakland by white policemen. There was a shootout and one white officer was killed. Newton was wounded and sent to jail. Prosecutors asked for the death penalty and a battle ensued.

"Free Huey" became the watchword for a generation trying to bring about racial reform. For many, the call for Newton's death rekindled memories of a racist southern justice that was just beginning to crumble. For white students, it was a lever that tilted them toward massive guilt about their "white skin privilege."

In late March a representative of the Black Panther Party came to speak at one of our CCAS meetings. He asked us to come to a rally that Friday in Oakland in support of Huey Newton. I volunteered to represent the group.

The Black Panther Party had been founded by militant blacks who had grown up mostly in the Oakland ghetto. They viewed themselves as black revolutionaries. Their founders, Bobby Seale and Huey Newton, had been strongly influenced by the radical black author Frantz Fanon. Fanon's form of Marxism, more relevant to blacks than that of Marx, Lenin, or Mao, helped create a model for an organization the two men formed. They called it the Black Panther Party.

The Black Panthers scared the living daylights out of most white people. First of all, they had really serious uniforms. Black trousers, black leather jackets, and black Castro-like berets. The most serious part of their uniform, however, was the guns they carried. The Panthers carried guns in the streets—and it was legal.

Don Mulford, the conservative Republican from Berkeley, freaked and introduced legislation to prohibit the Panthers from carrying guns in public. The Panthers decided to pay a call on the California state legislature to lobby against the bill. Newton, Seale, and about twenty friends actually walked onto the floor of the California Assembly, carrying loaded handguns, rifles, and shotguns. Suffice it to say, their protest was duly noted.

The police wanted Huey P. Newton's ass, and they'd caught him, which is why the Black Panthers were now holding a rally in support of the "brother."

The Panther who gave me a ride there was dressed all in black and wore huge dark sunglasses. At seven-thirty at night, in raining and murky weather, I didn't have great confidence in my pal's ability to see the road. But I hopped into his car and we exchanged the obligatory, very complicated soul handshake.

The guy was totally wasted. He had been smoking dope all day, he said, in preparation for the rally. He handed me the biggest joint I had ever seen. It must have been rolled with a toilet paper roll. I took a hit and almost choked to death. He thought this was hilarious, as did the three other black-clad Panthers in the back.

As we drove toward Oakland I expected that we would talk about revolutionary movements in the third world or how long-disenfranchised blacks were getting political power. Wrong. We were four guys getting stoned and cruising around. What we talked about was girls.

Of course we discussed them from a radical perspective. One of the guys talked about Stokely Carmichael, the head of the Student Non-Violent Coordinating Committee (SNCC). "Stokely's got it right. See, he says the proper position of women in the movement is prone!" The brothers all slapped hands. The driver chipped in, "I heard a speech one of the brothers gave about 'pussy power' and he said Superman was a punk 'cause he never even tried to fuck Lois Lane." Everyone in the car thought this was the most hilarious thing they'd ever heard. I was really glad when we finally reached the rally.

A few notes about the rally: (1) I was one of about a dozen white people in a crowd of several thousand; (2) most of the speeches were about how white people are devils; (3) most of the calls for action were to do serious bodily harm to—you guessed it—white people.

I looked around and saw a lot of angry folks. A lot of angry folks with guns! I was betting big time on revolutionary solidarity between the races. This might have been a real bad idea.

Finally the rally ended. As they dropped me off, with the strains of "FREE HUEY! FREE HUEY!" still ringing in my ears, the driver reached into his coat and pulled out a button. He got a serious look on his face and handed it to me. To this day I'm not sure if I was supposed to be flattered or insulted. The button read: "Honkies for Huey."

BERKELEY

MAY 1969

*Never get into fights with ugly people
because they have nothing to lose . . .*
MY FRIEND ALAN

People's Park could be viewed either as a spontaneous movement of
the people of Berkeley to make a safe, green, improvement to their
community, or the reckless takeover of private property by an anarchist band of street freaks. It kind of depended on how old you were.

Located just a tear gas canister shot away from the university,
the park had been a three-acre muddy field the school had bought
a couple of years before. In mid-April a number of street people decided the field would make a groovy park. They decided to
reclaim the land from the university and give it back to the people. All this was to be done under the doctrine of squatters'
rights.

For the next few weeks, hundreds of students and street people,
folks who wouldn't work if their parents or employers begged or
paid them, worked for free at the park. They transformed the mud-
splattered field into a grass-covered park by bringing together a
weird collection of sod, shrubs, and seedlings. A grove of apple
trees was planted and a brick walkway was laid. Swings and a
sandbox for kids were put up; there was even a fishpond, and my
favorite feature, a "revolutionary cornfield," was planted.

People's Park became a very cool place to hang out. Architec-
tural critic Alan Temko gushed about it in *Newsweek,* calling it "the

140

most significant innovation in recreational design since the great public parks of the nineteenth and early twentieth centuries."

The only problem with the park was that the land it was built on belonged to the university, which had paid over a million dollars for it a couple of years before. It didn't take long for the grown-ups on the university's board of regents to notice that the kids had taken over their property, and with all the thoughtfulness of a Pavlovian dog responding to a juicy slab of meat, California governor Ronald Reagan and the regents reacted.

Berkeley's chancellor at that time was a perfectly decent man named Roger Heyns. Mr. Heyns got caught right in the middle of a classic lose-lose situation. To the radicals at Berkeley, People's Park was living proof that power could, and should, flow from the bottom up. In addition, they realized that it was a perfect opportunity to turn moderates, especially students, into radicals. They sensed that the park would create a fantastic opportunity for a confrontation with the authorities.

To Ronald Reagan the issue of the park was equally tailor-made for political gain. Here was a clear-cut chance for the aspiring presidential candidate to make a stand. The park was clearly an illegal takeover of the university's property. If the state of California let the kids get away with this, nothing would be safe. It was a perfect occasion for the governor to "unleash the dogs of war" and teach the kids about property rights.

Chancellor Heyns was more accountable to the board of regents than to the constituent student body. The regents wanted the kids out of the park; thus Heyns had to act. "We will have to put up a fence to reestablish the conveniently forgotten fact that the field is indeed the university's and exclude unauthorized persons from the site. That's a hard way to make a point, but that's way it has to be," he said. Sure enough, that same night, huge No Trespassing signs and a tall steel mesh fence went up. Everyone was pissed off.

The next day there was supposed to be a rally in support of Israel in Sproul Plaza. Microphones and a podium had been set up, and the poor Hillel Club members who were hosting the rally didn't know what hit them. Within moments their rally had been taken over by an ad hoc committee to save the park.

Various speakers ranted and raved about the injustice of taking the park away from the people. How could the university claim the land? Didn't it belong to the Native Americans before we were even born? A reverend grabbed the mike: "The spirit which built the park is stronger than gas or clubs. As followers of Jesus, we are committed to stand with that spirit—the spirit of the poor and alienated trying to create a new world on the vacant lots of the old." *Yeah!* screamed the multitudes. Other speakers compared the university taking over the park to the United States government trying to take over Vietnam. We all whooped and screamed for justice. Finally, of all people, the president of the Associated Students of the University of California grabbed the mike. I'm not sure if he meant to unleash us, but he screamed out at the crowd, "Let's go down and take over the park."

That was all we needed. We all began to chant "Take the park! Take the park!" Suddenly we were on the move, heading down Telegraph Avenue to liberate the park.

Thousands of us trotted toward the target. Crash! The front window of the Bank of America was broken. We were intoxicated by our own power. We ran headlong into a large group of police who guarded the park. A couple of kids turned on a fire hydrant and aimed the water at the cops. The crowd cheered. A few picked up rocks and tossed them at the police. The cops were not going to put up with that. Suddenly a massive barrage of tear gas was aimed at us. Wild in the streets again.

I retreated with most of the demonstrators back toward campus. Guess who was waiting for us? The blue meanies—and they were furious. Once again, they viewed us as a bunch of rich, privileged brats. It was weird, the working-class cops putting down the ruling class's kids who were trying to act like revolutionaries . . . such was America in the 60s.

Both sides had been through too many street fights. We were all angry and exhausted by the ritual. It was as if we were acting out a familiar dance. This all changed with the first shotgun blast.

The blue meanies lost it this time. They changed from firing tear gas to shooting shotguns loaded with no. 8 birdshot. They fired point-blank into the crowd. Kids went down.

I ran toward a guy I knew from one of my classes. He was grabbing at his hand, which was spurting blood. I helped him up. Part of his thumb had been shot off. I felt like I was in a war zone. I tried not to freak out as I helped the kid make it back to campus, where a first aid station had been set up. I turned the kid over to a white-jacketed guy I assumed was a doctor, and stood to catch my breath. My God, they were shooting at us. All we wanted was a place for kids to play—a park—and they were shooting at us.

Later that day I found out that some poor guy, James Rector, who'd been watching the riot while standing on a roof along Telegraph Avenue, was shot to death by the police. A couple thousand National Guardsmen arrived and a curfew was declared. The grown-ups had once again gone to war with their children.

A curfew had been imposed on the city, and as I snuck along the side streets to get to our CCAS meeting, I was as angry and alienated as I could ever remember being. We gathered at the small second-story room we called our clubhouse. In the distance we heard an unseen bugler playing taps. Tomorrow we would teach them not to mess with us.

BERKELEY

Violence is as American as cherry pie . . .
H. RAP BROWN

Pyotr Kropotkin was a nineteenth-century Russian anarchist who proposed that private property and unequal distribution of wealth should give way to the free distribution of goods and services by a cooperative society. After he died, mourners carried the black flag of anarchism at his funeral. We decided to name our brigade Kropotkin in his honor.

About a dozen of us had gathered at CCAS headquarters to come up with a strategy for how to confront the police the next day. A couple of the guys, Ted and Alfred, wanted us to arm ourselves. Everyone had seen some sort of atrocity committed by the blue meanies. Over a hundred kids had been shot and wounded. We were beyond angry. We wanted to take action.

The sociologist Robert Staughton Lynd once quoted a young radical: "After a certain amount of frustration you decide that at least you can make yourself into a brick and hurl yourself." We were ready to fling ourselves against the man.

We knew there would be demonstrations the next day. We decided that we would be part of the revolutionary vanguard and protect the people against the cops. Again Ted and Alfred suggested we come armed, but the rest of us shouted them down. We

144

couldn't beat the state with weapons, we argued, only with ideas and actions.

Ted was one of those kids who had to be best at everything he did; thus he was one of those "radical-er-than-thou"-type guys. He was a textbook case of what went wrong with the student movement and why it ultimately failed. Every discussion with Ted was a gut check. Every action was scrutinized for bourgeois attitudes. In short, the guy was a total drag to hang with.

The summer before, Ted had worked on the assembly line in a car plant in Michigan. It was part of his revolutionary consciousness-raising experience. He was going to bring his message of world revolution to the workers. Of course they laughed at him. They cared about overtime, not the plight of their third-world "brothers." After a couple of weeks Ted had been fired when he tried to lead his co-workers in a wildcat strike over the issue of shipping parts to South Africa. He proudly boasted about walking off the line chanting revolutionary slogans. Big surprise: None of his co-workers followed. I'm sure they viewed Ted the same way we did—as a total asshole.

Now Ted and Alfred were in heaven. They could take action. "The man has shown his true fascistic colors," they said. "We have to strike back. Create a confrontation in which nobody could sit on the fence. This is our chance to turn moderates and liberals into true believers." They went on to lay out a plan that would have sent all of us to prison for the rest of our lives. Molotov cocktails tossed into the Bank of America. Blowing up police cars. Throwing acid in pigs' faces. We all sat there amazed and enthralled by their enthusiasm and passion, sickened by their bloodthirstiness.

"The issue of violence to this generation is what the issue of sex was to the Victorian world," said psychologist Kenneth Keniston. Ted and Alfred were convinced the only way we could all shed our white skin privilege was to become outlaws. Tomorrow would be our chance. "Political power comes from the barrel of a gun," Ted quoted chairman Mao to us. "We have to show the man we're willing to die for what we believe in!"

I suggested maybe we could let air out of some of the police car tires. Ted called me a running dog lackey for the pig establishment. I called Ted an idiot. Soon everyone at the meeting was screaming at each other. All power to the people.

We all went home that night not knowing what the next day would hold for us.

As I walked into my apartment, my roommate frantically signaled for me to come to the phone. "It's Ramsey Clark . . . he wants to talk to you."

Ramsey Clark had been attorney general of the United States. His father had served on the Supreme Court. Ramsey, too, was consumed by what the war was doing to our country and had taken an active stand to do something about it. He had been invited by the North Vietnamese government to visit Hanoi to see our soldiers who were being held there as prisoners of war. A mutual friend had suggested that, because of my involvement with Dispatch News Service, I knew about the media and should be Clark's press secretary when he got back. Clark told me he'd be returning from Hanoi through San Francisco and wanted me to arrange a press conference for him. Sure, I said, I'd be glad to.

I hung up the phone and turned to my roommate. "So, ah, how do you think you give a press conference?"

The next morning we met at CCAS headquarters to prepare for the demonstrations. We all wore long-sleeve shirts and work gloves. We tied wet bandannas around our necks and put Vaseline on our faces to negate the effects of the tear gas the police would inevitably use. Ted had a pipe that he kept pounding into his gloved fist.

We headed over to the university, where a large crowd had gathered. Our plan was to work our way to the front of the group; then, when the police fired their tear gas, we would grab the canisters and toss them back. If the wind was in our favor we could hold the police off and defend the campus. Or so we reasoned.

Ted had also brought a bag of rocks along. He was going to "bean the bacon," by which I guess he meant hit a policeman in the head with a stone. I told him I thought that was a stupid idea. It would only incite them to retaliate against us. Ted gave me a condescending look and uttered the 60s equivalent of "duh."

After what I'd seen the day before, I was willing, as they say, to be just to the windward of the law, but I didn't want to get into a physical struggle with the police. That was a battle we couldn't win. They were too well armed and trained for us. Moreover, I was realistic enough to understand that armed struggle in the United States was a no-win situation for everyone. But there I was, joining the others in letting out piercing *Battle of Algiers* war whoops and taunting the police.

I believed that some kind of change had to take place. I knew the war was wrong. I knew that racism was wrong, I knew that exploitation and prejudice were bad, and so did all of the rest of the people with whom I demonstrated. What we didn't know was how to change things, so we did what we thought we had to do, and we stood at Sather Gate, chanting and yelling and demanding our park back.

Within half an hour of our arrival the police fired their first barrage of tear gas and charged. I and some of the other members of the Kropotkin brigade ran forward and picked up the canisters and began tossing them back. The crowd behind us started to panic and run. Suddenly there were only about a dozen of us throwing canisters back at the police. I looked behind me. Ted had run off with the crowd. I wasn't surprised. (In Stephen Ambrose's wonderful book *Citizen Soldiers* he points out that during the World War II most of the GIs who were boastful and had big mouths in training camp turned out to be cowards once the shooting started . . . things don't change.)

The police then did the one thing that was absolutely not in anyone's best interest. They drove us off campus and into the streets. Dumb idea. We couldn't do much damage at the University, but in town it was easy. Now we were in the business district of Berkeley. Windows were shattered, cars set on fire.

I remained at the front of the crowd. It was around this time that I met a great-looking woman. She was impressed with my outfit. I talked and acted like a real streetfighting kind of guy and when the next attack came I tried hard to impress her.

The blue meanies stormed down the street, firing tear gas canisters at us. Mr. Big Shot, I'd bragged to her about seeing a lot of street action in the Chicago riots and at the third world liberation confrontations. I knew what to do. THUMP! A canister landed right in front of us. Showing off, I bent down, picked it up, and hurled it back at the police with all my might. The woman looked at me with newfound admiration.

Then another barrage took place; another canister hit nearby. I rushed over to it, bent down to pick it up, and became completely awash in C2 gas. I had picked up the wrong end of the canister. I was drowning in tear gas. I got one last glance of the woman shaking her head and running away before I went down on my hands and knees, eyes blinded, throwing up. A real streetfighting man.

I'm not sure who saved me, but somebody grabbed me and dragged me to an alcove in front of a store. I curled up and tried to breathe. I'd never been in such agony. Fortunately, the police passed me by. I lay there for what seemed like hours, trying to regain my physical well-being. My eyes stung like crazy. I couldn't open them. I also had wretched everything I'd eaten for the last two weeks out of my system. I sat there, curled into a ball, moaning softly.

I must have fallen asleep, because when I opened my eyes it was dark. The streets were empty. I struggled to sit up. Suddenly I heard a group of men heading toward me. Coming down the street, marching three abreast, were the National Guard. A company of them walked over to me and stopped. One of them stooped to check me out. I pulled myself to my feet, looked at him, and smiled. I said, "Hey Joe, you got gum?"

BERKELEY

Suspense in news is torture . . .
JOHN MILTON

For the next two weeks Berkeley was occupied territory. We were not allowed to meet in groups of three or more or to be out past 10 P.M. The police and National Guard were everywhere and street demonstrations and spontaneous creations of new People's Parks erupted all over the city. I tried to stay involved, but the combination of having made such an ass of myself and the police's decision to use live ammo drove me back to class.

About this time Ramsey called me from Manila and said he'd be arriving in San Francisco the next morning. Was everything set? "Um, sure," I replied. Actually, I had found out a bit more about how to arrange a press conference. All you had to do was call the Associated Press and put your information on the day wire. What I didn't understand was that was the way you announced a meeting of the local garden club. What I had was the front page story of the world. The former attorney general of the United States had gone behind enemy lines and met with American prisoners of war. This was big news.

I called one of the editors to whom I had sold our Dispatch stories at the *San Francisco Chronicle* and mentioned that Ramsey Clark was coming back and asked him if he wanted to send a reporter over to meet with him. The editor went ballistic. "When's Clark coming in? Has he spoken to the prisoners? Does he know if the North Vietnamese have offered to come back to the peace table?" I began to realize how far over my head I was. I had to get organized.

I drove to the airport and somehow talked my way in to meeting the responsible adult in charge. I told him about Ramsey showing up the next morning and asked him for his advice about scheduling my alleged press conference. Fortunately, the guy had done this before. He booked a private room for us and set up a podium for microphones and stuff. He even gave me the phone numbers for most of the local media.

The next morning I headed out to the airport an hour before Ramsey was due to arrive. It was a media zoo. There were about a hundred reporters—all three networks, local TV stations, and radio stations.

When they found out I was in charge they pounced. If I'd give CBS an exclusive they'd lead the evening news with it. NBC told me they'd already been promised an exclusive. The UPI guy literally got me in an armlock and told me he'd destroy me if I didn't get him to Clark while he was still on the plane. I fled to the airport security lounge.

Ramsey landed and I met him at the gate. There was a stampede to get to him, but my airport buddy had set up barrier of security guards to protect him. Ramsey waved to the press and announced that he'd be with them in a minute. That minute stretched out to almost an hour. Much to his credit, Ramsey was not going to talk to the press until he had personally called the families of each of the prisoners he'd visited in Hanoi.

I kept walking out to the press room to tell the reporters that Ramsey would be there any minute, but it did no good. They were like ravenous beasts waiting to be fed. Expletives were hurled, threats were made; some crews even pretended to pack up and leave, but nobody went anywhere. They wanted to hear what Ramsey Clark had to say.

Finally he emerged. Clearly, he was physically exhausted from the flight and emotionally drained from talking to the prisoners' families. He cleared his throat, gave a short statement, and said that he would give full details at tomorrow's press conference. Tomorrow's press conference?

Ramsey turned and began to walk back into the security lounge. One of the reporters yelled out, "Where's the press conference being held?" Ramsey smiled and pointed at me. "Talk to David." Every eye in the room turned to me. As I slowly began backing toward the lounge, I experienced the first of the many *klungs* that I would have in my professional life. That's when all of your vital organs try to exit your throat simultaneously. I bowed to the reporters and ran for the lounge.

Fortunately, I was able to get it together and the next day we had a press conference in a rented room on the University of California campus. It was the same day the People's Park protests reached their boiling point and Governor Ronald Reagan decided it was time to take off the gloves.

As Ramsey took questions from the press, we heard the dull rumble of an approaching helicopter. Soon the noise was deafening. As we all rushed outside to see what was happening, the chopper let loose a cannonade of tear gas. They were spraying the campus. The first barrage fell neatly upon the assembled press, sending them gasping and swearing back into the room. I became somewhat hysterical, pointing at the sky and yelling, "See! See! That's what we're fighting! That's what we're up against." Anyway, I was convinced that we had raised the media's consciousness about the people's struggle. As I said, I was very young.

———

Working with Ramsey convinced me that academia was not the right place for me. Having had a taste of the real world, I couldn't go back to the library. I decided to quit school and take my struggle to the belly of the beast. I moved to Washington.

Baby David. This kid was to see more changes in his generation than all previous generations combined.

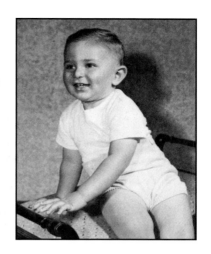

High school graduation. I enjoyed the pomp, but the only circumstance I cared about was that I was still a virgin.

David and friends, 1966.

*First love.
Yu Lin and I before
we were tragically
torn apart.*

*Every baby boomer's nightmare.
The A-1 classification meant
you could be called
for action in Vietnam.*

SELECTIVE SERVICE SYSTEM
NOTICE OF CLASSIFICATION

David___NMN___OBST
(First name) (Middle initial) (Last name)
Selective Service No.

| 4 | 118 | 46 | 7 |

is classified in Class ____1-A

until _____

☒ by Local Board,

☐ by Appeal Board

vote of _____ to _____

☐ by President

NOV 5 1965
(Date of mailing)

(signature)
(Member or clerk of local board)

David Obst
(Registrant's signature)

SSS Form No. 110 (Revised 5-7-63)
(Approval not required)

Jerry Rubin, Ed Sanders, and Abbie Hoffman, founders of the Youth International Party. As my grandmother would've said, they were a bunch of characters. (AP/Wide World)

Protests during the Democratic national convention in Chicago, August 1968. Grown-ups, instead of sending us to our rooms, sent us to hospitals. (AP/Wide World)

Protesting the closure of People's Park in Berkeley, 1969. This was not a good time for business at Shakespeare & Co. (AP/Wide World)

Black Panthers demonstrate for the freedom of their leader, Huey P. Newton. Many of us became honkies for Huey. (AP/Wide World)

Seymour Hersh, premier investigative journalist of his generation, did not score well in the category of "works well with others." (AP/Wide World)

William "Rusty" Calley was convicted by the U.S. army of killing 102 women and children at My Lai. As punishment, he was sent to his room. (AP/Wide World)

Carl Bernstein, Bob Woodward, and Deep Throat. (AP/Wide World)

Robert Redford, Dustin Hoffman, and Deep Throat. (AP/Wide World)

Daniel Ellsberg, leaker of the Pentagon papers. Helping Dan resulted in my having to flee the country. (AP/Wide World)

Leni Riefenstahl, czarina of Nazi moviedom, posed for the first cheesecake cover of Time *magazine. (AP/Wide World)*

Why is this man smiling? Richard Nixon says good-bye after resigning the presidency. (AP/Wide World)

I became friends with Clinton through Derek. Once I happened to be jogging at the same time as the president on the beach at Santa Monica. "Hey, David! Do you want to run with me?" Clinton shouted. "Sure, Bill," I said. "But what about Gore?"

Jane and I. My reason for getting up in the morning.

My Lai

By the end of 1969 there were more than six hundred thousand troops in Vietnam. Richard Nixon had been elected president. During his campaign, he had repeatedly sent secret messages to the leader of the South Vietnamese government, President Thieu, not to agree to any terms at the Paris peace talks that would help the Democrats. Nixon's attempts to undermine peace talks were nothing short of treasonous.

Now Nixon was in charge of the most unpopular war in United States history. American planes had already flown more than a hundred thousand attack sorties against the North Vietnamese and dropped two and a half million tons of bombs. Nixon promised a new policy of Vietnamization of the war, but none of us had any confidence that the killing would stop.

Grown-ups kept telling us about the domino theory: that pulling out of Vietnam would be an open invitation to the

*world communist conspiracy to go after each of the other
countries of Southeast Asia. Laos, Cambodia, and Burma
would fall, as would Korea, Japan, and eventually America.
We didn't buy it. Why did we have to go halfway around the
world to die for something that didn't make sense?*

*That fall The New Mobilization Committee to End War in
Vietnam demanded a moratorium on the war and hundreds
of thousands of men, women, and children marched on
Washington. A month later the president was forced to
surround the White House with DC Transit buses parked
bumper to bumper to protect the executive mansion from
hundreds of thousands more anti-war demonstrators. That
our species walked on the moon for the first time that year or
that a supersonic jet called the Concorde flew across the
ocean in record time didn't seem to matter nearly as much as
the war.*

*Nixon and his minions fought back. He called on what he
termed "the great silent majority" to speak up and voice their
support for him. But it was no use. He'd lost that most vital of
institutions—the media. U.S. newspaper and television
commentators assailed the president's handling of the war as
each night the horror of the conflict beamed into America's
living rooms. More and more of the establishment began to
jump ship and call for an end to the war. Again, Nixon struck
back. He unleashed good old Spiro T. Agnew, who attacked*

"an effete corps of impudent snobs—the dozen anchormen,
commentators, and executive producers who decide what
millions of Americans will learn of the world." A campaign
of intimidation against the press and television began and
immediately started to pay dividends.

As the 60s drew to an end, America was a bifurcated
culture. Marcus Welby, M.D. *competed with* Monty Python's
Flying Circus *for viewers.* Promises, Promises *with music by*
Burt Bacharach and Hal David, featuring the hit song "I'll
Never Fall in Love Again," played down the block from Oh,
Calcutta! *a review devised by Kenneth Tynan with scenes that*
included frontal nudity and simulated sex acts. "Raindrops
Keep Falling on My Head" was released at the same time as
"Lay Lady Lay." The Peter Principle, *one of the top-selling*
books of that year, demonstrated that employees tend to rise
to their level of incompetence, and, as if to prove the theory
right, The Saturday Evening Post *ceased publication after a*
hundred and forty-eight years.

Woodstock presented incontrovertible evidence that the
youth culture was a mass movement, while the murder of
Sharon Tate by Charles Manson and his hippie cult proved
that sex, drugs, and rock and roll weren't the answer. As I
reached Washington, the number of dead Americans in
Vietnam, almost thirty-four thousand, exceeded the number
killed in Korea. The cost of the war was running over twenty-

five billion dollars a year and was exerting tremendous inflationary pressure. A dollar I'd earned babysitting in 1958 was now worth only seventy-five cents. The war was pushing us into everyone's worst nightmare—an inflationary recession.

Yet the steepest cost of the war was not in money, but in the toll it took on our national spirit. Not since the Civil War had we been so divided a people. It was against this backdrop that I arrived in the nation's capital. For the next three years, trying to end the war would be my full-time occupation.

WASHINGTON

NOVEMBER 1969

I gave them a good boy
and they made him a murderer . . .
MOTHER OF ONE OF THE SOLDIERS AT MY LAI

In 1969 Washington still had a small-town feel to it. The New Frontier had brought some sophistication to the capital, but it was still a sleepy southern city. I arrived in the late fall and moved into a big house with Derek and a bunch of other kids from California. It was communal living without the group sex. We were politicos.

I had driven East, stopping in every major city along the way to see the managing editors of the local newspapers, trying to sell them Dispatch News Service. By the time I reached Washington I was 0 for America. Not a single paper had signed up to use us.

Fortunately there now existed an underground press in America, and they loved our stuff. A number of big-city alternative newspapers, along with about fifty college dailies and weeklies, subscribed to Dispatch. We were making just enough to stay in business.

In 1665 Sir Isaac Newton was forced to leave Cambridge because of the threat of plague and spent the summer in a small country cottage in Woolsthorpe. During the twenty-third year of his life he formulated the corpuscular theory of light, inventing the field of optics; developed his general laws of gravitation; and incorporated his concepts of time and infinity to create calculus. During the twenty-third year of my life I learned to hit backhand and met Seymour M. Hersh.

159

Sy was a good-looking bundle of energy from Chicago who scored poorly in the category of "works well with others." He had been Pentagon correspondent for the Associated Press, was Eugene McCarthy's press secretary, and had written an interesting book about chemical and biological warfare. Fiercely independent and unable to keep any opinions or emotions to himself, Sy was the classic loner.

We first met as tennis buddies. Since neither of us had a real job, we could sneak off to the courts whenever we wanted. Between sets we'd schmooze. One day Sy told me about a story he was working on. He'd gotten a tip from Geoff Cowen, then a reporter for the *Village Voice*, about a lieutenant in the army who had been charged with killing hundreds of "oriental human beings" (the army's language, not mine). Geoff felt the story was too important to be buried in the *Voice*, so he passed it along to Sy.

Sy nosed around and found out the rumor was true. The Pentagon had brought charges against some guy for killing a bunch of Vietnamese civilians. I said big deal, it happens all the time, our guys can't tell the difference between the Vietcong and noncombatants. Sy insisted this was different. The casualty count was over a hundred and most of dead were women and children. This was a big story.

For the next week I was like a little kid pulling on his daddy's pant leg. "Can I have it? Can I have it? Can I have it?" Sy was trying to sell the story to the mainstream media, but so far they had all passed. Finally, The *New York Review of Books* agreed to run it. I was crushed.

Out on the court again the next day, I could tell something was wrong because Sy's serve sucked and twice, after missing easy shots, he threw his racket. When he retrieved it the second time he pointed at me and yelled, "Okay, it's yours, but don't screw it up!" Bob Silver, the editor of the *New York Review of Books,* had pushed Sy too far and he'd pulled the piece from them. It was mine, and what a story it was.

My Lai was like a frozen frame in the tragic movie that was the Vietnam War. It was the American Malmedy. What was a company of heavily armed, angry, and frustrated young American boys doing on the northeast coast of South Vietnam's Quang Ngai province in the first place? They were there as part of a program called the Strategic Hamlet Program, also known as "pacification" or "rural reconstruction." The strategy was to move rural families into fortified hamlets and then drive the Vietcong out of the area. American military strategists had read Mao Zedong and understood that in guerrilla warfare the guerrillas are the fish and the people the sea. They had decided to catch the fish by removing the water. The orders were simple. Move the people out, kill the Vietcong. The program, like most of the war effort, was a total failure. There were just too many people. You couldn't just uproot the entire countryside and install the population in compounds. The people didn't want to leave. These were their ancestral homes. Someone had to grow the crops. Finally, it was impossible to tell the good guys from the bad guys. A man or woman working in a rice field might smile and wave to an American soldier during the day and lob mortars into his camp at night.

The job of pacifying the particular patch of countryside known as My Lai fell to the newly formed Americal Division. Within this division was the ill-fated First Battalion, 20th Infantry's Charlie Company. Led by Ernest "Mad Dog" Medina, the men of Charlie Company had volunteered to serve in Vietnam; only a few had gone to college. Most were between eighteen and twenty-one years old. One of their platoons was led by a boyish-looking five-foot, three-inch, twenty-four-year-old second lieutenant from Miami, William L. Calley Jr. Everyone called him Rusty.

Calley and his men had been in country for a while. They had been involved in a series of fruitless search-and-destroy missions and were taking far too many casualties. A letter home from one of the guys from Calley's unit, Gregory Olsen, a devout Morman from Oregon, summed up their anger and frustration:

Dear Dad:

How is everything with you?

I'm still on the bridge we leave here Saturday for the mission [for My Lai].

One of our platoons went out on a routine patrol today and came across a 155-mm artillery round that was booby trapped. It killed one man, blew the legs off two others, and injured two more.

And it turned out a bad day made even worse. On their way back to "Dottie" [camp] they saw a woman working in the fields. They shot and wounded her. Then they kicked her to death and emptied their magazines in her head. They slugged every little kid they came across.

Why in God's name does this have to happen? These are seemingly normal guys; some were friends of mine. For a while they were like wild animals.

It was murder and I'm ashamed of myself for not trying to do anything about it.

The isn't the first time, Dad. I've seen it many times before.

Saturday we're going to be dropped by air in an N.V.A. [North Vietnamese Army] stronghold [My Lai].

I love and miss you and Mom so much . . .

Your son,
Greg

The next day, Greg and Charlie Company entered the small village known as My Lai. The killing started without warning. Advancing slowly through the hamlet, one of the younger members of Calley's platoon took a civilian into custody and then unexpectedly stabbed the man in the back with his bayonet. The man fell to the ground, gasping for breath. The GI then killed him with another thrust of his weapon.

The floodgates were opened. My Lai became a killing field. The soldiers shot anyone and everyone. Most of the victims were women, children, or old men. A couple of samples from Seymour Hersh's report on the day:

About eighty people were taken quietly from their homes and herded together in the center of the village. A few hollered out, "No VC. No VC." Calley left Meadlo and a few others the responsibility of guarding the group. "You know what I want you to do with them." he told Meadlo. He came back ten minutes later. "Haven't you got rid of them yet? I want them dead. Waste them." Meadlo followed orders. He stood ten feet away from them and then he and Calley began shooting them. There are seventeen M16 bullets in a clip of ammunition. Calley and Meadlo each used close to four or five clips each. Women were huddled against their children, vainly trying to save them. Some continued to chant, "No VC." Others simply said, "No, No, No."

A lot of women had thrown themselves on top of the children to protect them, and the children were alive at first. Then the children who were old enough to walk got up and Calley began to shoot the children.

One further incident stood out in many GIs' minds: seconds after the shooting stopped, a bloodied but unhurt two-year-old boy miraculously crawled out of the ditch, crying. He began running toward the hamlet. Someone hollered, "There's a kid." There was a long pause. Then Calley ran back, grabbed the child, threw him back in the ditch and shot him.

Charlie company left almost five hundred dead Vietnamese in My Lai. They reported their action to headquarters as a courageous victory over the Vietcong. They claimed an enemy body count in the hundreds. Their apparent victory did not go unnoticed. A few days after the battle, General William C. Westmoreland, then commander of United States forces in Vietnam, sent the following message: "Operation Muscatine [the code name for the My Lai assault] contact northeast of Quang Ngai City on March 16 dealt the enemy a heavy blow. Congratulations to the officers and men of Charlie Company for outstanding action."

When Sy told me I could break the story, he'd already meticulously begun to put it together. The result was one of the great sagas of investigative journalism. Using his sources in the Pentagon to track down Calley's lawyer, Hersh flew to Salt Lake City to meet the man and confirmed the fact that the Army had brought charges against Lieutenant Calley. His next stop was Fort Benning, Georgia, where, despite the military's best efforts to hide him, Hersh found Calley. Sy spent an entire evening with the accused man and got confirmation of the tragedy that had been My Lai. This was the story that Hersh had given me to run with. It was now my job to convince the editors of America that it was newsworthy.

Once again I hadn't a clue as to what I was supposed to do, but one of the great things about being young and inexperienced is that I didn't care. I got a copy of a book called *The Literary Marketplace*, which listed the names and phone numbers of all of the newspapers in America. I opened to A and began calling. It wasn't until I got to the Cs that I got a hit. The *Hartford Current* in Connecticut said they were interested and requested a copy of the story. Oops. In my enthusiasm to sell the story I hadn't really thought out how I was going to get it out. I couldn't just mimeograph it and mail it like I did for our Dispatch stories: it would take three days to reach the *Current*. In a panic I ran down the block to Sy's house; thank God he wasn't home. Forget it, I'd figure out how to send it later. I had to sell it first. I began to improve my sales technique. "Yeah, I'm pretty sure the *Boston Globe's* going to run it—yeah, okay, I'll send it to you at the *Chicago Sun-Times*." "Yeah, I'm pretty sure the *Sun-Times* is going to run it. Okay, I'll send it to you at the *Globe*."

"Yeah, the *Globe* and *Sun-Times* are probably going with it . . . I'll send it right out," and so on. Like Blanche DuBois, I have often relied on the kindness of strangers. One such stranger was Howard Simons, then managing editor of the *Washington Post*. Howard told me to send the story over. Unlike most of the men I'd spoken to that day (I'd been on the phone for nine straight hours and had yet to speak to a woman), Howard was more interested in me than the story. Who was this kid trying to get onto his front page? We started to chat. I told him about Taiwan and Culver City. He invited me to have lunch with him. I really liked him. Finally, I bucked up my courage and asked, "How do I send out the story?" There was a long silence and then Simons began to laugh. He laughed a bit longer than I thought was polite, but finally he said, "Send it out by telex. It'll get here within the hour." A telex was a teletypewriter that could send copy over phone lines. I thanked Howard and ran over to Sy's house again.

Sy was in a rather agitated state. He was still working on the story, badgering sources in the style that was to make him the top investigative reporter of his generation, and he didn't want to be bothered. I told him that I thought things were going well and that I'd be sending the story out to about fifty papers—by telex.

Sy jumped out of his chair, grabbed me and slammed me against the wall. "Telex! How are we going to afford to send fifty telexes! It'll cost a thousand bucks!"

"Telex collect?" I gasped. He let go of me.

"Oh. Good idea. Now leave me alone. I've got to finish this if we're going to have it for the AMs." I ran back to my house and got back on the phone.

Late that Wednesday afternoon, November 12, I drove down to the Western Union office to send out our story. The piece began:

Lieutenant William L. Calley, Jr. is a mild-mannered, boyish-looking Vietnam combat veteran with the nickname of 'Rusty.' The Army says he deliberately murdered at least 109 Vietnamese civilians during a search-and-destroy mission in March, 1968, in a Vietcong stronghold known as 'Pinkville.'

Pinkville was the name assigned to My Lai because the hamlet appeared as a pink blot on the platoon's military maps. That night, Sy and I anxiously waited for the first edition of the *Washington Post* to arrive at a newsstand near the Mayflower hotel. We had sent the story out, but we had no idea if anyone would run it.

The papers arrived and there on the front page was Sy's story—with a *Washington Post* reporter's byline. They had taken our story and assigned it to one of their own guys. We went nuts, but when we calmed down we were both slightly elated. The story was out. The army couldn't cover it up any longer. America would finally know what horror that had been visited on the lost souls of My Lai.

The next morning Sy and I met at the National Press Building. The Press Building is kind of a clubhouse for the nation's reporters. Most out-of-town papers keep offices there for their Washington correspondents. On the top floor of the complex is the library that subscribes to papers from all over the country. Sy and I stood in the stacks waiting. Finally, the out-of-town papers began to come in.

"It's in the *Sun-Times!*" I shouted across the room. "On the front page!"

"The *Bulletin* has it above the fold!" Sy yelled back.

All in all, over fifty papers ran our story that morning. Almost every major paper in the United States. The notable exception was the *New York Times*.

That Sunday night Sy came over to my house. We were both wondering what to do next—how to follow up. The story had run on Thursday, but it didn't have as much of an impact as we had hoped. *Newsweek* and *Time* both ignored it. We were looking over the ways the various papers had played the story, most of them on page one, when Sy spotted another story in the *Washington Post*. It was an item about a guy named Ronald Ridenhour who had announced that he was responsible for initiating the army's inquiry. Sy jumped out of his seat and began yelling, "The kid! The kid! The kid!" Suddenly it all made sense to Sy. He hadn't been able to figure out why the army would air its dirty laundry about the killings. Why had the army charged Lieutenant Calley? Ridenhour was the answer.

Sy got on the phone and tracked the kid down. He planned to take the first flight to Los Angeles to meet Ron, now a student at Claremont College.

But now we had a problem: Sy and I were broke. I was living hand-to-mouth off Dispatch and Sy was a freelance writer. Between us, we barely had enough cash to cover airfare to California, and Sy's credit card was close to being maxed out. Somehow we managed to get him on the flight and I began calling people for help. My father immediately wired us some money, but it wasn't nearly enough. I called a number of people I'd worked with in the anti-war movement and one of them suggested I call Stanley Scheinbaum.

Stanley was a remarkable man whose heart was on the people's side of almost every issue, and he happened to be rich. He had had the good sense to marry Betty Warner, a talented artist and warmhearted woman. Betty had had the good sense to be born an heiress to the Warner Brothers fortune. They were a formidable pair. Stanley, a university economist by training, had put his money where his brains were and boosted Betty's already considerable nest egg into a genuine fortune. What was even more remarkable about Stanley and Betty is that they were willing to share the wealth. They didn't just write checks, but dove into causes with a shared passion to change the world for the better.

I got hold of Stanley and didn't get halfway through my pitch. "How much do you need?" he demanded. I told him and the money was in Sy's bank account by the end of the day. Sy would be able to continue to pursue the story.

He flew to L.A., got a car, and drove out to Claremont. He caught Ridenhour between classes and took him out to lunch. Ridenhour had served in Vietnam. When he heard about the massacre he wrote to the Pentagon, his congressman, anyone he could think of to make the army investigate what happened in My Lai. His persistence paid off. One of the main reasons the army had brought charges against Calley was because of Ron. He was also a gold mine of information. He knew who all the players were and where to locate them.

For the next two days Sy raced across the country interviewing members of Charlie Company. He began writing on the plane home. By the time he reached Washington we were ready to go. I rushed again to Western Union and sent the story to the world. I spent the next ten hours on the phone.

This time the story had an impact—but not in America. I sold the story to the *London Times*. They had played it big. Huge head-lines. It became the most important story in the world to the English, even pushing the news of the second moon landing off the front page. THE STORY THAT STUNNED AMERICA, headlined the conservative *Daily Mail*. The *Daily Sketch* was even more provocative. In a front-page editorial they wrote that "Americans were dragged down to the level of terrorism practiced by the Viet-cong. From today the Vietnam war is over . . . the President will have to pull out." A group of demonstrators staged a noisy protest over My Lai in front of the American Embassy, and the issue was debated on the floor of the House of Commons. Even the *New York Times* could no longer ignore the story.

Joe Eszterhas, who would later gain great fame as a screen-writer of overpriced, underthought screenplays, was then working as a general assignment reporter for the *Cleveland Plain Dealer*. He received a phone call from a schoolmate, an ex-GI named Ron Haeberle, who said he had photographs of the massacre. Joe got the photographs into the paper and they shocked the country. One picture of a line of women and children lying dead in a trench became one of the most famous photographs of the war. The My Lai story now had a life of its own.

Sy kept going. He found more soldiers who had been at My Lai. They all wanted to talk. Finally he ended up in New Goshen, Indi-ana, at the home of Paul Meadlo. Paul had been next to Calley during the worst of the killing spree. Paul had loaded clip after clip into his M16 and shot women and children. Now he was will-ing to go public and tell all.

Sy called me, terribly excited—we had the front page story of the world.

As a typical baby boomer, I instinctively knew that nothing was real in America until it was on TV. I picked up the phone and called *CBS Evening News*. I told them what we had and they wanted it—badly. When I told them that we needed our expenses covered, they hesitated. "We're not into checkbook journalism," said the *CBS Evening News* managing editor. I politely asked him for NBC's phone number. He asked me where I wanted the check sent.

Sy brought Paul Meadlo to New York. On the way he wrote another installment of the story and we sent it out for morning release to all of our papers. This time I didn't have to call them. I knew they'd run it.

CBS had put me up at a nice midtown hotel. Sy came over to visit. The phone rang moments after he arrived. It was Abe Rosenthal, head man of the *New York Times*. I'd sent him a copy of our story figuring they'd have no choice but to run it. It was too big a story to ignore and they were America's paper of record. Mr. Rosenthal couldn't have been nicer. He complimented me on the great job Dispatch and Seymour Hersh had done on uncovering the story. I beamed. Sy, on the other hand, was frowning and pacing the room. Rosenthal continued his banter and then casually mentioned that since the *Times* was the paper of record, he'd kind of like to have one of his reporters come over and interview our star witness. Sy grabbed the phone out of my hand.

"Mr. Rosenthal, it's Sy Hersh. Listen, you want an interview with Paul Meadlo? Well, he's somewhere in New York—find him." Sy slammed the phone down. I stared at him in awe. He'd just hung up on "all the news that's fit to print."

Seconds later the phone rang again. Sy grabbed it.

"Mr. Hersh," Abe Rosenthal yelled, "do you know who I am!"

"Yes," replied Hersh and hung up on him again.

That night Paul Meadlo led the *CBS Evening News*. Mike Wallace interviewed him and Paul calmly told America how he had shot women and children in the ditches of My Lai. It sent a shudder through the nation.

WASHINGTON, DC

DECEMBER 1969

Evil is easy and has infinite forms . . .
BLAISE PASCAL

I really thought our story would end the war. At the huge moratorium march that month I saw a number of people carrying signs saying REMEMBER THE PINKVILLE 109. Others simply pasted the gruesome pictures from the village onto placards. I couldn't imagine how, now that we had managed to freeze-frame this grisly moment of the war, any rational person would let it go on. I was wrong.

Lieutenant William Calley was found guilty by the military of having murdered twenty-two Vietnamese civilians and was sentenced to life. Then an amazing thing happened. Overnight, he became an authentic American hero. The first tip-off came in early December. American Legion members in Columbus, Georgia, home to Fort Benning, took out a four-column advertisement in the local paper proclaiming support for Calley. They accused the media of trying to "tear down America and its armed forces." From there the movement snowballed. A group of American Legion posts announced plans to raise a two-hundred-thousand-dollar defense fund for Calley. The lieutenant was granted permission to leave the stockade and attend fund-raisers. He was treated like a hero.

Governor George Wallace of Alabama came out for Calley. They met in Montgomery, Alabama and Wallace told the press that he was "proud" to meet Calley, then added: "I'm sorry to see the man tried. They ought to spend the time trying folks who are trying to destroy this country instead of trying those who are serving their country. I've been shot at myself and there's nothing like it." Calley stood next to him beaming.

Members of Congress began reading their support of Calley into the *Congressional Record*. Many of them accused us of perpetrating a "massacre hoax" on the country and warned that the news media were engaged in a game of psychological warfare against the American people.

Viking Press paid Calley a hundred thousand dollars for the rights to his life story, and perhaps the most shocking of all, a record called "The Battle Hymn of Lieutenant Calley" sold almost a quarter of a million copies:

> *My name is William Calley, I'm a soldier of this land,*
> *I've vowed to do my duty and to gain the upper hand,*
> *But they've made me out a villain,*
> *They have stamped me with a brand,*
> *As we go marching on.*

But the most obscene reaction to Calley came from the White House. Richard Nixon, who seemed to have no compunction against playing politics, even with war crimes, decided that popular opinion was on Rusty's side. He ordered Calley to be released from the Fort Benning stockade and put under house arrest in his comfortable apartment. So what if a few Vietnamese got shot? As the song said, Rusty was a little boy who wanted to grow up and be a soldier and serve his country. Because mail to the White House ran a hundred to one in Calley's favor, it was far more prudent for the president to protect the lieutenant than to make an example of him. So what if Calley tossed two-year-olds into ditches and shot them? He was one of ours.

WASHINGTON

It is better to be making the news than taking it . . .
WINSTON CHURCHILL

The high of being in the center of a media firestorm was incredible.

Overnight I went from being a left-wing alternative media radical to a responsible journalist. Amazing what one good story can do. *Newsweek* did a story about us called "Hip Pocket AP." *Time* did a two-page spread hinting at secret, nefarious "Red" financing of our operation (we should be so lucky). Best of all, the *National Enquirer* named me as one of their Young Achievers of the Year. It was a great high, but how to sustain it?

I decided to make Dispatch into a serious investigative news service. With Sy as the quarterback and three or four other good reporters working with him, we'd shake up the county. I quickly got commitments from three well-known establishment reporters. They loved the idea of getting to do in-depth investigative work.

I got a number of investors to commit almost five hundred thousand dollars to pay for the start-up costs. I traveled to Chicago, Detroit, Cleveland, and St. Louis and got commitments from their editors to carry Dispatch. It was going to happen. Our plan was to provide papers throughout America and the world with ten to twelve stories a year. Each one would be a front-page, above-the-fold story. Papers would pay a yearly fee to have exclusivity in their territory. I called my friend Howard Simons at the *Post* and

173

asked him out to lunch. He thought our idea might work, but he had reservations about the management—which was me. Good point. I was all of twenty-three and had no experience in either the newspaper or business world. So? Newton hadn't any experience in calculus before he invented it, I countered. Okay, bad example. "Hey, Howard, how'd you like to run it?" I asked. "You could leave the *Post* and . . ."

Simons held up both hands in surrender. Then he laughed and changed the subject. "Did you send in your Pulitzer nomination for Hersh?" he asked.

"Huh?"

"The Pulitzer? You've heard of it, haven't you?"

Of course I had. It is the highest award in journalism. What I didn't know was that you had to apply for it. I thought they just gave it to deserving journalists.

"What am I supposed to do?" I mumbled.

"Jesus, you haven't done it yet!" Now he was angry.

I shook my head. "When's the deadline for nominations?"

"Today, schmuck. I'm a judge on one of the panels. Christ, Hersh is going to kill you." Howard began to laugh.

I jumped to my feet. "But if it's postmarked today it's still okay, right?" I pleaded. Howard finished his drink and nodded. I ran out of the restaurant, stopped and dashed back to Howard. "What's got to be in the nomination?"

"Copies of the stories and a letter to the Pulitzer committee as to why you think your organization or reporter should be awarded the prize." Howard answered.

I reached across the table, shook his hand, and ran back to our house.

As luck would have it, a wonderful woman named Nancy Wynn Craig had moved into our commune. That month she was working with me.

I rushed into the house and told Nancy my problem. It was a little after three and the post office closed at six.

Nancy tore back to the National Press Building and went to the library. She began making copies of Sy's My Lai stories. On the way home she bought a huge, oversized binder for us to put them in. Meanwhile, I was writing up the nominating letter for the Pulitzer committee. Everything I wrote sounded horrible. Finally I gave up and wrote in longhand that the stories spoke for themselves.

Nancy finally returned to the house with her stuff. It was a little after five. She looked at my letter with disdain, but there wasn't time to do anything about it. We put the stories in the huge binder and then frantically looked around the house for something to wrap it in. We found some old Christmas paper. It would have to do.

"What's their address?" she asked me.

"Damn!" I ran for the phone and called Howard. He wasn't in. I called information; there was no listing for Pulitzer. I remembered that Pulitzer used to own the paper in St. Louis. I called St. Louis information. Nothing. It was now 5:45.

I called Howard's house. He wasn't home, but I got one of his daughters. I asked her to look around her father's desk and see if she could find his address book and then look up Pulitzer. Nancy and I stood waiting as she went to look. Minutes continued to tick away. Finally, she came back on the line.

"I couldn't find it," she said.

I was starting to panic.

"But I found a letter to daddy from them. Maybe you could use their return address?" she asked. What a brilliant little girl. Made sense, her dad was a genius.

She dictated the address, which I wrote in longhand onto the Christmas paper.

Nancy had the car warmed up and waiting.

I ran from the house and dove in. Nancy drove like a hellion through Washington, DC rush hour traffic. It was 5:55. We got stuck at a red light. She ran it. We neared the post office and Nancy executed a brilliant and highly illegal U-turn and I was off.

I made it into the building with two minutes to spare. Sy's Pulitzer nomination was on its way.

For the next couple of months I continued to put our news service together. More and more papers were expressing interest. I also approached one of the networks and one of the newsmagazines. They too said that if the price was right they would subscribe. I was beginning to think we might just pull this off.

Late one afternoon I got a call from Howard Simons.

"Are you sitting down?" he asked.

"Yeah, why?"

"Your guy won the Pulitzer. It'll be announced tomorrow." He laughed.

I let out a yelp, thanked him, and took off to tell Sy.

I burst into his office. "Sy, you won it! You've won the Pulitzer."

Sy jumped up from his desk and rushed at me. He picked me up and slammed me against the wall.

"Don't fuck with me!" he screamed.

"I'm not, you idiot. Put me down. You won! Howie Simons just called me. . . . You won!" I screamed back at him.

Sy let go of me, collected himself, and headed back to his desk.

"Yeah, well, they were great fucking stories," he mumbled and went back to work.

A week later I was in the National Press Building in downtown Washington going over a two-year lease with the manager when Sy walked in and asked to talk to me. He suggested that maybe it wouldn't be such a smart idea to sign the lease. Something had come up . . . he'd gotten an offer from Abe Rosenthal to be chief investigative reporter at the *New York Times*. My idea for a news service was over. Without Sy we couldn't do it. *Klung* #2.

Pentagon Papers

*In 1971 the average United States taxpayer gave the
government seven dollars for medical research, thirty dollars
to explore outer space, forty dollars to build highways, and
one hundred twenty-five dollars to fight the war in Vietnam.
Many didn't think they were getting their money's worth. To
help pay for the war, the government got into the numbers
game and off-track betting was created. That year, American
imports topped exports by over two billion dollars, the first
time we'd run a deficit since Grover Cleveland was president.
President Nixon raised the price of gold and the dollar was
devalued by another 8.5 percent. Wall Street loved it and the
Dow made record leaps upward on record volume sales. The
largest union in the country, the AFL-CIO, complained that
they had absolutely no faith in the ability of the president to
successfully manage a war economy. Nixon responded by
imposing a ninety-day freeze on United States wages and*

prices, by temporarily suspending the conversion of dollars into gold, and by demanding of Congress an import surcharge. All of this was to try and strengthen a dollar that was being torn apart by the inflationary pressures of the Vietnam War.

That year the Twenty-Sixth Amendment was ratified, lowering the voting age from twenty-one to eighteen. We had pointed out to the grown-ups that if we were old enough to fight for our country we should at least be allowed to vote for the idiots who were sending us three thousand miles to die.

The women's rights movement gained tremendous momentum. Ms. magazine was born bearing the manifesto, "Eliminating the patriarchal and racist base of the existing social system requires a revolution, not a reform." President Nixon replied, "Let me make one thing perfectly clear. I wouldn't want to wake up next to a lady pipefitter."

Nineteen seventy-one was the year the Food and Drug Administration told us that dining on swordfish was kind of like eating a thermometer. (They're both full of mercury.) Cigarette ads were finally banned on radio and television, but cigarette sales broke all existing records, with over five hundred fifty billion sold that year. Rolls-Royce went bankrupt. The United States gave up building the SST (supersonic transport) and conceded the market to the Concorde. It then went into the strip-mining business and began extracting over a trillion tons of soft coal in the northern Great Plains.

The movie business had fallen on hard times. Major studios were putting out fewer pictures, but independent productions were starting to happen all over the country. Sexually explicit films had lost their box office appeal and Stanley Kubrick's A Clockwork Orange, *Robert Altman's* McCabe and Mrs. Miller, *Woody Allen's* Bananas, *William Friedkin's* The French Connection, *and Peter Bogdanovich's* The Last Picture Show *were the big hits of the year.* Sticky Fingers *by the Rolling Stones, "Country Road" by John Denver, "If Not for You" by Olivia Newton-John, "Imagine" by John Lennon, and "Theme from* Shaft*" by Isaac Hayes topped the charts.*

Jim Morrison, the Doors' lead singer, and rock guitarist Duane Allman bid a farewell to the living.

Bury My Heart at Wounded Knee *by Dee Brown gave us a shocking account of the destruction of American Indian society.* Honor Thy Father *by Gay Talese showed us the inside workings of organized crime, and John Updike, Bernard Malamud, and Herman Wouk each published new novels,* Rabbit Redux, The Tenants, *and* The Winds of War, *respectively.*

On the tube, All in the Family, The Flip Wilson Show, Marcus Welby, M.D., *and* The Mary Tyler Moore Show *turned in impressive Nielsen ratings. The three networks, after much whining, finally agreed to limit prime time to 8:00 to 11:00 P.M.*

Richard Nixon had promised us he was going to end the war. Now, near the end of his first administration, that war continued unabated. By the summer of 1971, I, along with countless others, was becoming angry, frustrated, and desperate to bring the war to an end.

BOSTON
JUNE 1971

It is one thing to show a man that he is in error,
and another to put him in possession of the truth . . .
JOHN LOCKE

Suddenly I was jobless. I kept sending our stories from Vietnam out, but it wasn't the same. I'd seen the real thing . . . I didn't want to go back to the mimeograph machine. I was kind of at loose ends—then I met Daniel Ellsberg.

All groups have hierarchies. Whether they're rodeo stars or insurance brokers, there is always a pecking order. Because of My Lai I had become a big shot in the antiwar movement. A lot of people brought me stories, ideas, schemes, and plots to help stop the war. Most of them were either too stupid or too violent to be taken seriously. Daniel Ellsberg, however, was to be taken very seriously.

A deep, brooding presence, Dan was way too smart for his own good. Driven to excel at everything he attempted, be it the piano, Harvard, the marines, or the Defense Department, Dan had to be the best. He'd gone to Vietnam a gung-ho, win-at-all-costs hawk, a man who was willing to lead charges down Vietcong underground tunnels. And then, as his brilliant mind realized the folly of our involvement, Ellsberg decided that he must risk all to end the war. His stealing of the Pentagon Papers from the Rand Corporation was a brave and desperate act. Ellsberg felt that if the American people

181

knew the truth about how our leaders had planned this war, they'd be sickened and demand its end. I agreed with him and was willing to help in any way.

On June 13, 1971, the *New York Times* published the first installment of the Pentagon Papers. These were highly classified documents the Defense Department had put together to trace the history of the Vietnam War. After two more installments of the papers were published, the Nixon government obtained a temporary injunction and further publication of the documents by the *Times* was halted in federal court. Shortly thereafter I got a call from Dan asking if I could meet him ASAP in Cambridge, Massachusetts. I caught the next shuttle to Boston.

Dr. Ellsberg might have been on an incredible high, but he was also scared to death. He'd gone into hiding, moving into the Fenway Motor Inn along the Charles River in Cambridge under a fictitious name. The *New York Times* had been in possession of the papers for almost three months before running them. The *Times* had not told Dan the story was going to run that Sunday and he'd left copies of the Pentagon Papers all over the country. He needed someone to collect them. I quickly volunteered.

For the next ten days I crisscrossed America picking up hidden copies of the papers. This was no easy task. For one thing, *The History of the U.S. Decision-making Process on Vietnam Policy*, as the Pentagon Papers were formally known, was an immense document, almost three thousand pages long. For another, Dan wasn't sure where he'd left all of the copies. I'd go to Chicago, pick up a copy, come back to Cambridge, go to San Francisco, pick up a copy, and come back to Cambridge, and then Dan would remember he'd left a copy in his marine footlocker in L.A. Organizational skills were not his strong point.

It was while I was in Los Angeles that I made a serious tactical mistake. Dan had left his footlocker at Bekins Van and Storage in

Santa Monica. To get possession of the footlocker, I had to sign for it. Cleverly, I used my real name. Within hours after I took the papers the FBI showed up at Bekins. I was in a heap of trouble.

I took the footlocker back to Cambridge, checked into a hotel, and waited for Dan to contact me. The problem was that now Dan was seriously underground. Sidney Zion, a former reporter for the *Times*, had gone public to reveal that Dan had been the source of the leak of the papers to the *New York Times*. For the next two weeks the FBI sought Ellsberg for questioning. Dan was able to successfully evade them and continue orchestrating the dissemination of the Pentagon Papers to various newspapers.

Every time the government thought it had stopped Dan from getting the story out, he'd slip the papers to another newspaper. He gave them to the *Washington Post*. The government got an injunction to keep the *Post* from publishing. Dan gave the papers to the *Boston Globe*. The government enjoined the *Globe* from publishing, so Dan gave the papers to the *St. Louis Post-Dispatch*. The government took the *Post-Dispatch* to court. The next day the papers were in the *Chicago Sun-Times*. The editor of the *Boston Globe*, after hearing that FBI agents were searching locations in Cambridge where the papers might be hidden (that being with me), panicked and hid his copy of the Pentagon Papers in the trunk of a car in an unlit parking lot in downtown Boston.

While Dan was playing his game of cat and mouse, always just one step ahead of the Nixon rats, I was sitting in the Cambridge hotel room, bored out of my mind. That's when I decided to jimmy the lock on Dan's footlocker.

When Dan finally emerged I turned over the extra copies of the papers to him. We talked about his future. He knew that the government was going to go after him hard and he would need the financial resources to defend himself. I offered to help him get a book contract. That could be a fast and easy way to get money.

By this time, I kind of knew about the book business. After My Lai I'd gotten calls from a number of publishers asking if we wanted to turn the stories into a book. Sy, already having a publisher, quickly made a deal without my help. But I was interested in finding out how the book business worked, so I went up to New York and met with a couple of publishers. Suddenly I was an agent.

Dan and I put together a rough proposal, and I waited for him to turn himself in. I knew that his fifteen-minute window was coming up and that our timing was crucial. On June 28 Dan surrendered to the United States attorney in Boston. On the same day he was indicted in Los Angeles on two counts of converting government property to personal use and of illegal possession of government documents. Later, the same grand jury would hand down new indictments adding twelve criminal charges, including conspiracy, theft, and violation of the Espionage Act.

It was around this time that the maverick democratic senator Mike Gravel of Alaska entered the picture. Gravel had moved to Alaska from Massachusetts to make his fortune. As a highly successful real estate developer, he'd made more than he ever could hope to spend and then moved on to politics. He'd been elected the year before to the Senate and had become frustrated by his inability to get anything done. He didn't understand the rules of the club and was treated as an outsider. He was sick of the war and had lost a great deal of respect for the institution of the United States Congress. Ellsberg sensed he'd be the right guy to slip the papers to.

Dan's plan was for Senator Gravel to read the papers on the floor of the Senate. Under the rules of that body, Gravel would have congressional immunity, and since the papers would then be part of the public record, any newspaper in the country would be allowed to run them. It was a great safety net for Dan in case the Supreme Court ruled against the *Times*.

The senator decided that he was going to set the record for the longest filibuster in United States history by reading the entire Pentagon Papers into the record. Reasonable estimates put the time required for this at about thirty consecutive hours. With television cameras rolling, Gravel began to read. He went on and on and on and became almost as famous as Ellsberg. It was wonderful grandstanding and continued to get the papers into the public consciousness.

A few days after he finished reading the papers, I got a call from Senator Gravel. He wanted to make sure that the Pentagon Papers would be accessible to the public. He wanted to publish them as a book. Ellsberg had told him I knew about the publishing business and recommended me to help him out.

I'd never been in the Senate before. Gravel gave me a personal tour of the building and sneaked me onto the chamber floor. The room was impressive. Deep leather seats . . . the podium . . . the gallery . . . very lifelike. Some old guy—I think he was the official usher for the Senate—came in and found us and politely asked us to leave. Apparently, they'd been having problems with late-night visitors from some of the other Senate staffers. They were bringing women onto the floor and consummating in the chambers. The janitors had complained to the ushers about having to clean up after them.

I told Gravel I thought the papers would make a great book. I set up a meeting for the next day with Dick Snyder, the president of Simon & Schuster books.

The senator and I flew up to New York on a Thursday to arrange publication of the papers. Our plan was to produce a single volume of the work. Though it would be the size of an average telephone book, around eight hundred and fifty pages, Simon & Schuster agreed to do an initial printing of almost a quarter of a million copies.

Gravel went back to Alaska and I holed up with Simon & Schuster's lawyers to work out the financial terms. There was one slight caveat: We had to let the board of directors of Simon & Schuster examine the papers before the deal was formally approved. But this was just a mere technicality.

As we negotiated the deal I suddenly realized that my commission on the books would net me roughly three times the combined earnings of everything I'd ever made in my life, and because we were going to accelerate the book's production schedule, I'd have the money within a month.

It was a strange feeling to suddenly be confronted with that kind of dough. I'd lived in a commune, didn't own a car or even a television. I finished working out the terms of the deal and took the contract back down to Washington for Senator Gravel to sign on Monday.

That Friday night I was with Senator Gravel's staff helping prepare an introduction to the book. We finished and sent the copy by courier up to New York. The book was finished. It would be on the presses by Sunday and hit the streets early next week.

I went back home and told the other members of my commune what had happened. I told them I was suddenly going to come into a shitload of money, and I wanted to share it with the group. I'd need some of it to pay my expenses and keep Dispatch going, but I wanted to give the rest to the Movement. (Those were the days.) I think I might have even quoted Francis Bacon: "Money is like muck, not good except to be spread."

Better to be nouveau than never to have been rich at all. We argued heatedly about where the money should go. One of the guys suggested we give it to The Institute for Policy Studies, a new-left think tank in Washington that supported a number of men and women who were trying to change society. Another wanted the money to go to the Environmental Action Committee, a group of cutting-edge activists who fought corporate America in the trenches. Some argued for it to go to the anti-war movement, others the civil rights movement, or to Cesar Chavez and his people. Pretty soon the discussion was out of control. The money had subtly shifted from being mine to being the commune's, and everybody had a proprietary interest in how it should be spent. There is nothing uglier than listening to a bunch of radicals arguing about money. People were screaming at each other. Friendships were dissolving as I watched. It would have been amusing if it weren't so sad.

Around midnight I got a call from the lawyers at Simon & Schuster. Bantam Books had just released a paperback edition of the *New York Times* copy of the Pentagon Papers. It was selling like crazy. There was no room in the marketplace for two books. The Simon & Schuster board had vetoed the project. They were pulling out of the deal and the Gravel edition was dead. I stood there for a moment in shock. *Klung* #3.

I walked back into the living room. One cute little blonde woman was screaming her protests at a tall, shaggy-haired guy's suggestion. He wanted to give the money to the Institute because they could more effectively use it to work change within the system.

"Fuck working within the system!" she yelled. "When I see a hundred top corporate executives in jail—in the same cells, with the same guards, cellmates, and shit that blacks and longhairs have to take—*then* I'll believe the system's worth trying to save!" The guy shook his head.

"I think we should send the money to Huey and the Black Panthers," said the girl. The room exploded.

"Fuck that! Give the money to Cesar. Viva la huelga!"

"No! No! We've got to stop the war! Until we stop the war nothing's going to matter!"

I tried to get the group's attention, but everyone continued to yell. Finally I let out a very cool wolf whistle. (I'd been practicing in the backyard.) Everyone shut up.

"Listen up," I said. "There's no money. They've pulled out of the deal."

Total silence for a beat.

"Yeah, but what if he had gotten the money?" said the cute blonde. "What would we have done with it?"

And they were off again. It was way too much fun to stop. I smiled and went up to my room.

WASHINGTON

AUGUST, 1971

Get out of the way of justice. she's blind . . .
STANISLAW JERZY LEE

Daniel Ellsberg had become the most discussed man in America. His picture was on the cover of both news weeklies. He drew crowds wherever he went. People either loved him as a hero for exposing the government's lies about the war or hated him as a traitor who was giving aid and comfort to our enemies. It was time to sell his book.

Actually, I didn't have to do much. I got a call from an editor of one of the major paperback houses in New York asking for the rights. He made a preemptive offer of an obscene amount of money and I accepted.

Dan was very pleased with the deal for a couple of reasons. To start with, he knew he'd have tremendous legal fees to pay. (In fact, they neared a million dollars.) In addition, the publisher wanted to rush the book out, which pleased Dan because he would then be able to have his side of the story on the public record.

I went to New York and worked out the final details and brought the contracts to Cambridge for Dan to sign. The book was going to be a collection of Dan's papers on the war, connected by intersti-tial essays by Dan explaining his conversion from a hawk to a dove. Because of the timeliness of the book, we were on an incred-ibly tight deadline.

189

Back in the chips again. The commune once again took up the debate as to how to spend my newfound wealth.

For the next two weeks I called Dan on a regular basis to see how he was doing. He assured me he'd finish with time to spare. He had collected a number of papers, the centerpiece being a brilliant treatise he'd written for the American Political Science Association the year before. In that piece, titled "Escalating in a Quagmire," Ellsberg pointed out that the ultimate discrepancies between the presidential policy and the policies recommended by Kennedy's advisors were not that great and that, in fact, Vietnam was a "President's War." Dan felt that no American president, Republican or Democrat, wanted to be the one who lost the war—especially before an election. In essence he was saying that our leaders took us in there with their eyes wide open and led tens of thousands of helpless young men into the quagmire of Vietnam.

A week before the publication date I got a panicked call from the publisher. They had not yet received anything from Dan. I got on the next plane to Cambridge.

Dan sheepishly admitted that he hadn't finished the book. (In fact, he hadn't started it.) As the most famous man in America that month, everyone wanted to speak with him. He'd been interviewed repeatedly, been on all the talk shows, been asked to lecture. He was a very busy guy. I offered to sit down with him with a tape recorder and have him dictate the few pieces we'd need to put between the papers he'd already collected. We tried it.

Dan started speaking about his experiences in Vietnam. Before long he was in tears. The guilt he felt about his complicity in our country's Vietnamese policy decisions, especially the pacification programs, was too intense for him to deal with. We had to stop.

Dan assured me he'd get it together. He'd never missed a deadline. He'd get the copy to the publisher. He promised that he wouldn't take any more meetings or go on any more talk shows. I had no choice but to believe him.

A week later I was back at my commune chairing yet another of our countless meetings on what to do with the money. I'd gotten the first half of our advance and wisely put it in the bank—after Gravel I wasn't taking any chances. I'd been trying to reach Dan for the last three days without success. The optimist in me pictured him hiding out in an undisclosed location writing his little heart out so as to make his deadline.

A Western Union messenger arrived at the door with a telegram. (Yes, they still sent them in those days.) It was from our publisher . . . the deadline for turning the book in had passed, the deal was off.

I went back in and told the group. They were starting to lose patience with me. I got on the phone and tried to reach Dan. I put in a call to his lawyer. Big mistake. The telegram was just the beginning of my problems.

BAGHDAD

OCTOBER 1971

*I have just returned from Baghdad. It is the only thing
to do if you find yourself in Baghdad . . .*
FRED ALLEN

Use immunity. Kind of has a nice ring to it, huh? However, when
a Boston federal grand jury granted it to me it was anything but
amicable.

The administration had decided to make an example of Ellsberg. To Nixon, stealing government secrets and giving them to
the press was on a par with exposing yourself to his daughters. The
full resources of the Justice Department would be used against
Ellsberg, and I was quickly caught in their web.

When I spoke to Ellsberg's lawyer, he told me that the grand
jury was going to issue a subpoena for me to appear before it, and
that I would be granted use immunity. What that meant was that
nothing I said before the grand jury could be held against me.
What it also meant was that I could not invoke my Fifth Amendment rights while testifying. I was screwed.

My options were:

1. Testify and tell the truth, thus implicating Ellsberg.

2. Perjure myself and risk harsh fines and a jail sentence.

3. Refuse to testify and be in contempt of the grand jury and go
   to jail.

A true lose-lose-lose scenario.

I did have one other choice: Flee the country.

Baghdad, ancient center of caravan routes, home of the Tower of Babel, nestled along the Tigris and Euphrates rivers, was a total shithole. But, it did have one thing going for it: It was in Iraq and Iraq had no extradition treaty with the United States. So that's where I ended up, with quick stops along the way in Cairo, Beirut, and Damascus. I figured if I kept moving I'd be safe. Only two flaws with that plan:

One, they weren't really looking for me.

Two, being an American Jew in Egypt, Lebanon, Syria, and Iraq was far more dangerous than facing a Grand Jury.

Once again, I was young.

I traveled about the Middle East for the better part of two months.

I went to Alexandria, Egypt with my friend David and his girlfriend. David's father had been in the foreign service, stationed in Beirut, so David could speak Arabic, and he knew his way around the Middle East. We arrived in Alexandria after a sickening (literally) sea trip from Naples. David and his girlfriend went to see a tacky Egyptian movie and I arranged to meet them at a bar later that afternoon.

At the bar, a somewhat seedy waterfront dive, a man motioned for me to come to his table. "You are to meet your friend here?" he asked.

I nodded.

"He'll be late. But sit down. Have a drink."

I sat with man and his friends for a while, drinking bad Egyptian booze and chatting it up. Turned out he was an Egyptian sea captain.

He told me he had a car and offered to show me the city. I had some time to kill, so I agreed. We hopped into his car, a late-model Ford, and began cruising the city.

After a while I noticed that we were heading away from town. He was driving along the coast, softly humming to himself. I asked him where we were going. He casually reached across the seat and put his hand on my genitals. WHOA! I quickly removed it. I began to explain about different cultures and stuff when he tried to grab it again. I pushed his hand away and he tried to grab my hand and put it on his member.

For some reason I had begun reading Mickey Spillane's *Mike Hammer* books on this trip, which probably explains my next act. I slugged the guy. Hard. In the face.

The car careened out of control and bounced up against the curb. I jumped out and ran all the way back to the hotel we were staying at. I told David and his girlfriend what had happened. They fell on the floor laughing. Nevertheless, I made them take the train that night to Cairo. I left all my Mickey Spillane books behind.

In Cairo, David's girlfriend had some kind of women's problem and went to see a doctor. She came back a couple of hours later, badly shaken. Her examination had been fairly routine, she said, but then the doctor had told her that he wanted to run a "special test" on her to make sure his diagnosis was correct. Would she please masturbate to climax for him?

David and I tried not to lose it, but we couldn't help it. We both burst out laughing. She charged David and began punching him. "I know! I know!" she yelled. "But he was a doctor, and listen! You two have to go to his office and beat the living shit out of him!"

We had no choice. I think she would have gone back to the States if we hadn't. David and I dutifully headed into downtown Cairo to teach the medical pervert a lesson. Thank goodness he wasn't in his office. We headed back and stood outside our hotel. David told me to punch him.

"Huh?"

"Come on, we have to at least look like we were in a fight," he said. I punched him in the arm.

"No, hit me in the face." This was getting ridiculous. I'd never hit anybody in my life, except my brother, and now for the second time in a week I was going to hit a guy in the face.

"Please. Otherwise she's going to split," David pleaded.

I gave him a tap on the jaw.

"Do it harder!" He pushed me.

I shoved him back. He slapped me. A group of Egyptians began to gather round us. I slugged him in the arm.

"No, you asshole, the face!" he screamed.

I let him have it. A perfect right cross, square to his lip. It started to bleed. The Arab crowd watched in wonder as David reached up and dabbed at his bloody lip.

"Thanks, man," he said and hugged me.

———

A week later I was flying alone from Cairo to Beirut. I stood in the reception area waiting for my flight when suddenly airport security grabbed me and threw me into a small room. Two incredibly tough-looking guys came in to interrogate me. I had no idea what I'd done wrong. They couldn't have known I was Jewish. Thank God, I wasn't carrying any hash. I hadn't even seduced any young Egyptian women to come live with me. They kept asking me if I thought my "little plan" was going to work. I had no idea what they were talking about. Finally I asked them which part of my plan they'd taken exception to. The uglier of the two pointed at my sleeping bag. (I was traveling with a backpack and sleeping bag so I could crash at youth hostels.)

"Why are you traveling with a parachute?" he asked.

"Huh?"

He walked over and picked up my nylon sleeping bag.

"You don't find it suspicious that a foreigner plans to get on a flight with our Minister of the Interior and he brings a parachute?" the man asked in his best Peter Lorre imitation.

I sighed, walked over to the backpack, and took out the sleeping bag. I unrolled it, opened it, and laid it on the floor. I got down and started to get inside of it.

"For sleeping," I said.

The two men left the room. Twenty minutes later they returned with an even uglier guy. He was wearing a really neat uniform, though. They motioned for me to show the new guy what I could do with my parachute. I got back into the bag.

Finally they let me go. However, just to be safe they confiscated my parachute/sleeping bag.

I wandered from Beirut to Damascus and then took an overnight bus from Syria to Baghdad. It was pretty cool. We left at midnight and drove all night across what seemed like endless stretches of dessert. We had to travel with our lights off because of the risk of bandits. I tried to stay awake to help the driver as lookout, but failed, and when I awoke we were in Iraq.

While on the bus I befriended a young Sudanese student who was going to work in the oil fields of Basra. I hung with him in Baghdad for a week or so. We went out to see the Tower of Babel in Babylon. This was reputedly where Noah's descendants had tried to build a very high tower and were prevented from doing so by a confusion of tongues or something. All that was left was a bunch of old stones with soft drink concessions around them. For the next week or so we took in the myriad of other tourist attractions Iraq had to offer. (Which was none.)

I went with the student to the southern port town of Basra and got the worst food poisoning I've ever had. He suggested I go to Kuwait to see a doctor.

Kuwait was about as weird a place as I'd ever been. An admixture of traditional Arab culture set against everything the almighty dollar could buy. These people were seriously wealthy. My Sudanese friend gave me the name of a pal of his. The guy was my age and his dad had just bought him a new Caddy. We spent the night cruising the main drag of Kuwait City.

While in Kuwait I got great news. Some idiots had broken into Ellsberg's psychiatrist's office and the judge had tossed the case out of court. I could come home.

A final note, just to close the circle. Years later I found out one of the reasons why Dr. Daniel Ellsberg was seeing a psychiatrist—he had writer's block.

Miami Beach

In the spring of 1972 a state court awarded the prize money for the Kentucky Derby to the second-place winner, Forward Pass. The winner, Dancer's Image, was disqualified because the horse had been given drugs before the race. However, the court went on to rule that Dancer's Image should still be considered the winner of the race. This was not the only bit of confusion America would have with drugs that year.

America had always been a drug culture. Even before the media discovered hippies, doctors were writing nearly two billion dollars' worth of prescriptions a year for pills. By the mid-70s we were awash in barbiturates, amphetamines, antidepressants, and hypnotics. In 1972 alone over eight billion amphetamines, or pep pills, were manufactured in America. Grown-ups called them soft drugs (as opposed to our hard drugs). Anyone who'd ever had a goofball (barbiturates laced with benzedrine) knew it was the other way around.

We were pretty sure that everyone our age took drugs. Acid rock groups like the Grateful Dead and Jefferson Airplane had turned taking trips into an art form. D-lysergic acid diethylamide, a.k.a. LSD or acid, made it into every city, town, and burg in America. Mescaline and a host of other synthetic compounds followed and soon kids all over the country were having their minds expanded, blown, freaked, and fried.

The real culprit, however, was marijuana, grass, maryjane, boo, or, as we all called it, pot. If you smoked pot, and it was virtually impossible not to if you were a college-age kid, then theoretically you were part of the counterculture. A conservative estimate by the United States Public Health Service put the number of teens smoking pot at that time at about twenty million—a lot of people breaking the law.

This was our parents' worst nightmare come true. Drugs to them had been something lower-class bums did out of desperation. When we started dressing and acting like those same bums, grown-ups all over America began to mourn the American dream. Our parents had survived the hardships of the great depression. They had seen real tramps—men and women who had been beaten by the system and had given up. There we were, their own children, emulating those hobos, exalting in their derelict lifestyle. "Look Mom, I'm a vagabond!"

*This was something that was our own. We'd invented the
drug culture. Turning on was a ball. Food tasted better, ideas
seemed smarter, sex was out of sight, everything was so damn
heavy. We turned on, tuned in, and dropped out. For one
brief shining moment we became flower children, which was
great—for about that one brief shining moment. Before we
knew it, the excesses of the culture turned on us and we
became, as Ed Sanders described it in his book* The Family,
"a valley of plump rabbits surrounded by wounded coyotes."

*But drugs ultimately proved to be an antidote to political
activism. By 1972 campuses were quiet again. Two years
before, at Kent State, a number of kids had been shot dead
by National Guard troops. Kids had been shown that the
grown-ups were willing to whip their butts. The war was still
on, but draft calls were down. Two-thirds of our troops had
been brought back home. Nixon was president. In a word,
politics sucked. Trying to change things was meaningless;
everybody ought to get stoned. Do your own thing and the
positive vibes you generate will make the world groovy.*

*Drugs turned kids into nihilists and anarchists. Anyway,
as Abbie Hoffman used to say, "a modern revolutionary
headed for the television station, not the street." If the kids
wanted revolution, they could see it on TV.*

*By now, the overwhelming horror of Vietnam had made
radicals desperate. They were tired of jargon. They wanted*

*action. They kept upping the stakes. There seemed to be a
bombing a day in Amerika. A group called the Weathermen
(named after a lyric from a Bob Dylan song, "You don't need
a weatherman to know which way the wind is blowing")
planted a bomb in the United States Senate.*

*This, of course, played right into Nixon's hands.
Ironically, just as we were starting to get widespread support
from the country for the anti-war movement, it was torn
apart by internal dissent. Many on the left felt that the drug
culture killed it. Some claimed that Timothy Leary (the
father of LSD) was a CIA agent and that the spread of
drugs was a government plot to deflect energy away from
overthrowing the racist, imperialist ruling class. (One wit
countered by replying, "Marxism is the opiate of the
unstoned classes.")*

*As I headed to the political conventions of 1972 it had
already been a strange year. President Nixon had traveled to
Beijing and met with Chairman Mao Zedong and Premier
Zhou En-lai, ending a silence that had existed between the
two countries since 1949. That same year, Nixon's meeting in
Moscow with Party Secretary Leonid Brezhnev had been the
first visit of an American president to the Soviet Union.*

Andy Warhol painted Mao *that year.* The Waltons *and*
M*A*S*H *were the top hits on TV.* Deliverance, The
Godfather, *and* Straw Dogs *gave us generous dollops of*

*violence at the movies and books by William Blatty (*The Exorcist*), George Higgins (*The Friends of Eddy Coyle*), and Michael Crichton (*The Terminal Man*) gave it to us at home.*

The top television show remained All in the Family, *along with* Sanford and Son, Hawaii Five-O, Maude, Ironsides, *and* The Waltons. *Time Life, subscription cable TV, and Home Box Office began broadcasting. Maude became pregnant and had an abortion; Hal Holbrook and Martin Sheen starred in* That Certain Summer *and introduced homosexuality to the boob tube.* Bridget Loves Bernie *was canceled, in spite of high ratings, because religious groups objected to its intermarriage (Catholic-Jewish) situation. The stars went on to marry in real life.*

When I showed up in Miami for the conventions the country was beginning to swing back to the right. Richard Nixon and his followers were riding the crest of a wave that would give them the weapons to lead the country against troublemakers such as myself. Fortunately, it was only a matter of time until they used these same weapons to shoot themselves in the foot.

MIAMI BEACH

JULY 1972

When I was younger I could remember anything,
whether it happened or not . . .
MARK TWAIN

I came back to America without any clear plan of what I'd do next. I kept Dispatch News Service going while abroad, but most of our users were now just college newspapers and the underground press. A magazine offered me a job to be its managing editor, but I didn't like the guys who ran it. Finally, there was the book business. I'd signed up a number of books before I'd left, but I still wasn't sure if that was the right occupation for me.

It was around this time that Dick Snyder, the president of Simon & Schuster, asked me to come work for him. After I'd returned from Kuwait, I had resold Ellsberg's *Papers on the War* to Simon & Schuster. Dick had handled the negotiations, and we'd gotten along very well. Shortly after that, Dick took me out to dinner and offered me a job. I'd never been offered a job before.

A weekly paycheck? Security? Sounded good . . . but some inner voice screamed NO! I told him I'd think about it.

I decided to put everything off until after the conventions. I'd used my Dispatch stationary to apply for press credentials. I figured, having won the Pulitzer and all, they couldn't turn me down. I was right. I got two full sets of credentials, including floor passes back from both national parties. On to Miami.

I'd never been to Florida. Really nice place in July, if you're an orchid or a mosquito. I wandered over to the Fontainbleau Hotel along the strip to pick up my credentials. The Fountainbleau, headquarters for both parties, is the kind of luxury hotel we'd all have to live in had Mussolini won the war. They'd taken tacky to its logical extreme and the place was almost elegant in its taste-lessness. I was impressed.

Across the crowded lobby I spotted a kindred soul: Richard Neville. Richard and I had met in Boston. He was friends with Ed Victor, an editor I knew at Knopf. (Ed went on to become a hot-stuff agent in London . . . if you've ever bought a book at an inter-national airport, he's probably getting a piece of it.) Richard was a mischievous demon of an Australian who, for the last few years, had been driving the grown-ups in London crazy. He'd founded a wonderful counterculture magazine called *OZ*. *OZ* would take great pride each issue in trying to provoke some establishment fig-ure in the United Kingdom to lose it. For example, Rupert the Bear is the English equivalent of our Bambi, or perhaps Winnie the Pooh. Richard and his boys had put cuddly little Rupert into the most overt sexual situations they could think of. People were not pleased. Richard was arrested and tried on obscenity charges. He became an infamous character in the British Isles.

Now he'd come to try his luck at offending people in the land of milk and honey. I immediately loved the guy. Richard's sense of fun had been perfected far beyond that of anyone I'd ever known. He was a true cultural anarchist.

Richard greeted me with a big hug. We went out and sat at the Fountainbleau's modest swimming pool (it was the size of Delaware) and shared a joint. He told me about this wonderful group of people he'd hooked up with and invited me to come over and play. I showed him my credentials and his eyes lit up. "We're going to have some fun with these," he smiled.

———

Marjorie was a hybrid between a new age earth mother and a sophisticated Philadelphia Main Liner. Her father had made pots of dough and had bought Marjorie what could best be described as a mini-mansion in Miami Beach after her first marriage went south. Located on fashionable North Bay Road, her house abutted Biscayne Bay. With its large swimming pool, huge ceilings, and many comfortable bedrooms, the house was perfectly suited for a successful Miami Beach attorney, proctologist, or accountant. It was even better suited for a group of freaks.

Marjorie's house was one long, continuous party and everyone came. Julie Christie lounged at the pool with Abbie Hoffman. Jack Nicholson argued politics in the living room with Tom Forcade, the founder of *High Times* magazine. The place was magic. I immediately checked out of my hotel room and moved in.

———

Our first order of business was seeing how stoned we could get. Everyone who showed up seemed to have brought some kind of stash, so it wasn't hard. We wandered over to Flamingo Park where the street people were crashing. Most of them were sleeping in the park and just hanging out, waiting to see if Miami was going to be another Chicago.

I came up with a great idea. Miami Beach is one of the premier retirement communities in the country, so I decided to form the "YENTA-YIPPIE COALITION."

We found a Xerox machine at the hotel and printed up leaflets to hand out at the park. "Make Chicken Soup—Not War!—Feed the Kids." It was a great success. By the third day, lines of old men and women were bringing borscht, flanken, knishes, and other delicacies to the park. They may not have agreed with the kids' politics, but they were still someone's grandchildren and the old folks loved feeding them.

While at the park I met a young, sorrowful-looking guy who had deserted the army. He wanted to turn himself in but wasn't sure how to do it. That night we had a long talk with him and he made up his mind to turn himself in, but he wanted to explain why he'd left the army. He was very troubled by the war and felt the government had lied to him and the country about why he was there. I had another idea.

The next day I found Stanley Scheinbaum, the man who'd helped us out with My Lai and was now a member of the California delegation, on the convention floor, and what a floor it was. Four years before, at the Chicago convention, the delegates had approved a Credentials Committee resolution calling for a reform of the process by which convention delegates were chosen. A quota system was adopted that had a profound effect on who would show up in Miami.

I was amazed that they'd let me in, let alone onto the floor. As I looked around I could see why. I didn't look all that different from a lot of the delegates. Eight out of ten were attending their first convention, a quarter were under thirty, and almost half were women and blacks. Stanley's California delegation had eighty-nine people who were on welfare.

As Gay Liberationists helped assure George McGovern's sure defeat by chanting, "Two, four, six, eight, we don't overpopulate," and "Three, five, seven, nine, lesbians are mighty fine!" I told Stanley about the kid I'd met in the park. I thought it would make great television if the kid turned himself in to the chairman of the California delegation. Stanley liked the idea and said he'd take it to his people.

That night a group of us headed back over to the Fountainbleau to meet with Stanley. He told me it was a go, and we made plans for the kid to use my extra set of credentials to sneak onto the floor.

As Richard, I, and a wonderful madman named Bobbie, who was Marjorie's boyfriend, left the hotel, Bobbie stopped in his tracks and pointed to the foyer. There hung one of the most breathtakingly tacky paintings we'd ever seen. It was a collage of Kennedys, each of the brothers represented in a series of headshots mounted against a black background.

"I've got to have that," declared Bobbie. Richard and I looked at each other.

Bobbie went up to the second floor and found a Cuban busboy. He explained in Spanish that he was to take the picture down. The boy shrugged, walked with Bobbie back to the foyer, leaned over, and pulled up the picture. Bobbie had taken a tablecloth off one of the dining room tables and had the boy wrap it around the picture. He explained to the young Cuban that he was taking the picture to be cleaned. He shoved a ten-dollar bill into the kid's pocket and ordered the boy to follow him.

We stood in front of the Fountainbleau waiting for our car, both of us in awe of Bobbie's chutzpah. Finally his Mustang convertible arrived and Bobbie had the kid put the picture in the backseat. As Richard sat on my lap we calmly drove away from the hotel.

When we got back to Marjorie's everyone was very impressed. We hung the picture in the living room and tossed about ideas of what to do with it.

One of the guys at the house, whose name was Fire (how come my parents couldn't come up with a cool name like that?), said we should cut the various heads off and paste them on the walls inside Mr. Toad's Wild Ride at Disneyworld. His was one of the better ideas.

Suddenly Richard ran into the room holding a radio. "Listen to this!" he shouted. An all-news-all-the-time radio announcer was speaking.

"The picture, the official portrait of the Democratic National Party, is valued at forty thousand dollars and is . . ." Richard turned off the radio and pointed at Bobbie.

"That's a felony! Anything over ten grand is a felony. They could put us away for years!" he said in a broken voice. Richard's brushes with the law had left their mark.

Bobbie just smiled as if he knew he wasn't going to the big house over a tacky painting.

"Get me a phone book," he commanded.

Someone found one in Marjorie's kitchen.

"What's the address of the Republican National Committee in Miami Beach?" Bobbie asked.

That night Bobbie loaded the painting back into the car, drove across town, and left it at the front door of the Republican head-quarters. As soon as he got home he called the *Miami Herald*. The next morning we were all amused to read an angry denunciation of the Committee to Reelect by the Democrats. Seems they were upset by the "childish prank" the Republicans had pulled. If they had only known what Messieurs Liddy and Hunt had in mind for them.

The next day I brought the army deserter into the Democratic convention. I parked him in a visitor's seat and went off looking for media. I found the floor correspondents for all three networks and told them when and where the kid was going to turn himself in. They all said they'd be there. I went into the press tent and told various reporters there as well.

At six o'clock that evening, prime television time, we brought the fellow to the floor. There was an immediate media stampede in front of the California delegation as the young man went on national television and told the American people why he and countless other soldiers were sickened by the Vietnam war. Nevertheless, he was a soldier and didn't feel right deserting, so here he was, ready to face his punishment. It was a very emotional moment.

We kept waiting for the police or FBI or somebody to come up and arrest the guy. We thought the pictures of his being dragged off the convention floor would be very newsworthy.

Unfortunately, no law enforcement body seemed to care. Soon the floor correspondents and reporters began drifting off to other stories. We didn't know what to do with the poor guy. He still wanted to turn himself in, but we didn't have anyone to whom he could surrender. Depressed, he sank into one of the seats in front of him. Immediately two armed guards grabbed him. His credentials didn't allow him access to the California delegation's seats. He refused to move and, much to his and our delight, they arrested him.

———

As much fun as the Democratic convention had been, I knew the Republicans would be even better. I contacted all of my friends and invited them to come stay at Marjorie's. Amazingly enough, most of them came . . . one of them even met his future wife there.

Friendship in our generation was much different than it had been for our parents. For one thing, because of the spread of mass media throughout America, we had all shared the same cultural experiences. All of us had watched Mary Martin as Peter Pan, had worn coonskin caps like Davey Crockett, had listened to the same Top 40 hits, seen the same James Bond movies, read the same books by J. D. Salinger. In short, we shared a cultural birthright. We could all wax nostalgic for a shared boyhood, even if we had lived it a continent apart.

We had all met in Washington, DC at a poker game organized by Charles "Detroit Louie" Firestone. Charlie was a young lawyer at the Federal Communications Commission who'd worked his way through Amherst as a wrestling instructor and the lead nonsinger in the folk rock group called Tangerine Charlie and the Flat Tires.

He'd gone on to law school and decided he wanted to work in media law. His razor-sharp brain and disciplined work ethic ideally suited his chosen profession. Charlie had a smile that started at his forehead and continued all the way down his face. He was a genuinely jolly guy even before he started to look like a middle-aged Santa Claus. One quick Charlie story: The two of us once went to visit a journalist buddy of ours. Unbeknownst to us, the buddy was having a going away party for Sally Quinn, who was taking off for New York to begin her ill-fated television career. Sally answered the door and stared horrified at the two of us. "What are you doing here?" she demanded in her snobbiest social arbiter accent. "Can't you see I'm having a party?" Charlie didn't miss a beat. He nodded, smiled up at her, and said, "I know, we were so hurt you didn't invite us we almost didn't come."

Taylor Branch was a good ole boy from Georgia who'd come to Washington to write. Brilliant, articulate, an amazing athlete, Taylor had the marvelous ability to be joyful and serious at the same time. A true wordsmith, he took enormous delight in filtering the human condition through his luminous mind and sharing his insights with the public at large.

John Rothchild, a Yale-educated southerner, had already, in his early twenties, begun to realize the absurdities of American civilization. Rather than despairing, John reveled in them and found them a constant source of exhilaration and amusement. Like Taylor, he was learning to communicate these impressions in finely honed, clever, incisive prose. The two of them worked at the *Washington Monthly*.

John Marks had worked at the State Department. John, having grown up around money, had a much better sense of patrician society than the rest of us. He'd turned his back on a life of privilege, but slight manifestations of his past kept dripping out. For example, he had somehow gotten together the money to buy a small farm out in the Virginia countryside that had become our weekend clubhouse.

Dorothy McGhee, who was known in our poker game as "Fingers," had been to the manor born; though she lived humbly in the same near-poverty as the rest of us, her father, the former ambassador to Germany, owned an impressive estate not two hours away. Dorothy was the most nurturing soul I'd ever encountered.

Danny Okrent was the smartest guy any of us had ever met—and one of the weirdest. He took enormous pride in his eccentricities. Danny was blessed (or cursed) with an encyclopedic memory: There was not a piece of music, trivia, baseball lore, or political minutia he couldn't identify. Utterly suave and sophisticated at one moment, he could be counted on to drool all over himself later.

Dorothy was living with Charlie but would leave him to go live with Taylor, who had just split up with his wife, whose sister Patty was to marry Charlie. Hey, it was the 70s.

Marks's farm was a bucolic spot nestled along the shores of the Rappahannock river in southern Virginia. A couple of hours by car from Washington, it was a wonderful place to spend quiet time. It was also a fantastic place to trip, and most of us experimented with whatever was around at the time. I was kind of the Johnny Appleseed of MDA, a synthetic mescaline-type drug that actually did give one a peaceful, easy feeling.

Our many days and weekends there were full of conversations, hikes, sports, swimming, and fun. We forged bonds that would hold our friendships together for the rest of our lives. I don't think any of us realized it at the time, but we were all using Marx's farm to take one last deep gulp of childhood before moving on to the responsibilities of adult life.

Okay, back to Miami. The Republican convention was actually going to be more like a coronation for Richard Nixon. To me,

Nixon was evil incarnate. I could forgive him for being against all the social and political programs I held dear, I could even forgive him for being "Tricky Dick," but what I couldn't forgive was the squandering of hundreds of thousands of young men's lives in the senseless slaughter that went on and on in Vietnam. I also didn't think much of his vice president. Spiro Agnew had proudly proclaimed, "If you've seen one city slum you've seen them all." The man was an opportunistic fool and the Gallup poll the year before had placed him third among America's most respected men, trailing only the President and Billy Graham. Considering what an idiot this guy was, that was a frightening statistic.

Although I kind of liked the fact that he was driving moderates into the hands of us extremists, I truly feared for the Republic with Spiro Agnew a heartbeat away from the presidency. Fueled by the poison pens of William Safire and Pat Buchanan, Agnew traveled the country inciting deep divisiveness. Calling all Democratic nominees "nattering nabobs of negativism" and "pusillanimous pussyfooters" or "troglodytic leftists," he was mean-spirited and full of hate and fury. Over and over he hammered at the same theme: Attack the kids, attack draft resisters, attack homosexuals, and lump them together with criminals, drug fiends, and sexual perverts. Rip the country apart for a few points in the polls. A truly evil man. (There being justice in the universe, Agnew was to suffer a severe karma kickback and have to leave his office and the planet a broken, humiliated man.)

Anyway, we didn't like Nixon . . . so what to do? Richard came up with what we thought at the time was a brilliant idea: Deny Nixon the podium for his acceptance speech. The plan was pretty simple. We'd use my press passes to smuggle a test tube filled with noxious chemicals onto the floor of the convention. The vial, being glass, wouldn't set off any alarms when I took it through the metal detector. Just as Nixon was about to give his acceptance speech, I would walk to the front of the podium and drop the test tube and Richard, behind me, would step on it. The fumes would waft up to the podium and the odor would be so rank that Nixon and his cronies would have to evacuate the hall. Great idea, huh?

Our friend Fire joined us and we began to put our plan together. We were excited. Okay, let's get organized. The first thing we needed was a piece of paper and pencil to write down all the stuff we had to get. Damn, stuck already. We were too stoned to get out of our lounge chairs at the pool to get them. We sat there trying to figure out where one got test tubes. "Test Tubes R Us," volunteered Fire, and we all cracked up.

"Screw the test tubes," said Richard. "What do we have to put in them to make a world-class atomic stink bomb?"

More of the group gathered to help out.

"Rotten eggs," said one of the most beautiful topless girls I'd ever seen.

"Yeah, right, how do you stick fuckin' rotten eggs up a test tube?" asked Fire.

"Sulfur," answered a long-haired kid that none of us had seen before. "You need something with a sulfuric derivative in it. That's what will . . ."

Fire jumped to his feet. "Who are you?" he pointed at the guy. "How do we know you're not some kind of pig trying to set us up!"

"Hey, man, chill," the guy said and got up and headed for the tank of nitrous oxide.

Unfortunately, at that moment, Carol, a wonderfully uninhibited woman who'd just come back from India with the first nose ring I'd ever seen, had passed the mask for the nitrous oxide tank to a fellow she'd picked up in the park. The boy, already flying, wrapped the mask around his face, took an enormous hit and fell backward into the pool, pulling the entire tank of nitrous in with him.

We fished the boy out. He was okay, but the tank stayed at the bottom of Marjorie's pool for the rest of the summer.

For the next couple of days we proudly told everyone about our plan to "fuck Nixon." Luckily we never made it out of the talking phase. One of the cast of thousands that was making Marjorie's his home that week was a very clever, albeit drug-fogged, lawyer named Spencer. Spencer had passed the Florida bar, but his work ethic was somewhat suspect. Like Jimi Hendrix (in Miami pronounced imi endrix) he seemed to constantly have a purple haze in his brain. However, for one bright, shining moment he was lucid enough to keep Richard and me out of prison.

"You guys really going to try and pull this off tomorrow?" he asked.

"Damn straight," we both answered.

"You ever read Voltaire?"

"Yeah, like in junior high," I answered, remembering Mr. Kargle's classroom.

"Voltaire said the secret of being a bore is to tell everything."

We stared at him, trying to figure out what he meant.

He smiled, "You guys are getting really boring."

"Fuck off," said Fire, who by that time had actually found a pad and paper and began to make a list of things we needed.

"Listen, you dickheads, ever hear of the Civil Rights Act of 1964?" Spencer asked.

"What about it?"

"If, by some miracle, you guys actually did get this cockamamie scheme together and do it, you would be in violation of that act, which states that any person or organization that knowingly denies freedom of speech or assembly to another through unlawful means shall be guilty of a felonious act and shall go to prison for a period of not more than ten or less than five years!"

"Yeah, well, how are they going to catch us?" Fire challenged.

Spencer laughed. "Is there anyone in Miami you idiots haven't bragged about this thing to?"

Richard and I looked at each other. Oh well . . . maybe next time.

———

We still decided to check out the convention hall. Using my passes we got onto the floor. This time we were greeted by not a few hostile stares.

Richard took out a loaf of Wonder Bread and began passing slices of it out to the delegates. Most of them, being polite folks, accepted the slices of white bread with a confused thank you. I think the irony of his actions was lost on them.

I wandered about the hall, awash in a sea of upper-middle-class Republicans, when all of a sudden there appeared Abbie Hoffman who had somehow also gotten press credentials from the Republicans. He gave me a big hug and whispered, "Listen man, avoid all needle drugs—the only dope worth shooting is Richard Nixon." He cracked up at his own cleverness.

"Stick out your tongue, man," he commanded.

"What?"

"Just do it. Come on, it'll help you deal with this nightmare."

Like a true imbecile I stuck out my tongue. Abbie slapped a glob of black goo onto it from a bottle he was carrying.

"What the . . ."

"Hey, you'll dig it, man. I promise," he beamed. He started to leave, then dashed back.

"Don't worry about these folks. We're going to have them for lunch!" He turned to leave but came back again.

". . . And sacred cows make the tastiest hamburger." He finally walked away, falling over himself in mirth.

Whatever he gave me hit at the worst possible time. I was standing in front of the hall and Nixon's name was being put into nomination. Forty-foot screens of his face began flashing down at me. Countless thousands of sworn enemies began screaming, "Four More Years! Four More Years!"—except I was hearing, "You're in Fear! You're in Fear!" If George Orwell had tried to script my worst nightmare he couldn't have done a better job.

I froze for a couple of moments, staring up at the giant Nixon head laughing down at me, then bolted.

I ran down the aisle, knocking people out of my way, exited the convention center and continued to run for miles until I somehow reached Marjorie's house. I ran through the house into the back-yard and jumped fully clothed into the pool. I tried to hide on the bottom, holding onto the nitrous oxide tank.

Luckily, "Fingers" McGhee was there and helped fish me out of the water. For the rest of the night she talked me down and brought me back to some semblance of sanity. By morning I was still shaken, but okay. By then I also knew it was time to move on. I was going to go West.

BERKELEY

We are the people of this generation,
bred in at least modest comfort, housed in universities,
looking uncomfortably to the world we inherit . . .
SDS PORT HURON STATEMENT

Bo Burlingham could have been a poster child for the American Dream. Bright, energetic, insightful, he'd been accepted by Princeton University to be groomed as part of the nation's elite. Instead, Bo became president of the school's SDS chapter and began plotting the revolutionary overthrow of the very aristocracy that had hoped to adopt him.

I'd met Bo in Boston when he was working as a staff writer for an underground paper, *Boston After Dark,* which was to become the *Boston Phoenix.*

Bo had gotten a job offer to become editor of *Ramparts* magazine. *Ramparts* was a radical, left-wing, counterculture monthly that had gained a following because of its hard-hitting investigative reporting into the transgressions of the United States government. *Ramparts* had been the first to expose CIA penetration of the student movement, for example, and had provided a home for a number of new and exciting writers.

Bo, his wife Lisa, and their newborn son Jake were packing for the trip to California when I came by their apartment, hoping to watch the Boston Bruins hockey game. Lisa wasn't too thrilled with Bo stopping his packing to watch the game, but I bought her off. I had a plane ticket to New York and I gave it to her in

218

exchange for letting Bo and I watch the last period. Afterward, I helped Bo finish packing and drove down to New York with him.

Our trip to New York quickly took on all the attributes of a bad Laurel and Hardy movie. We dropped furniture, we banged into things, and finally, Bo's poor car didn't have the horsepower to drag the trailer we'd loaded. Within a couple of miles it conked out and we had to rent a truck, reload all of his stuff, and tow his car down to New York.

Along the way Nixon resumed the bombing of North Vietnam and mined Haifong harbor. Once again the planet tottered on the brink of world war. We'd stopped at Bo's folks' house along the way and I remember, as I crawled into bed that night, having that same childhood feeling of dread I'd had in the eighth grade. Once again I was sure that the world, hence my life, was going to end. This time, though, rather than stay in bed (which would have really confused Bo's mom), I decided to do something about it. I offered to help Bo with *Ramparts*.

Bo thought it was a terrific idea. With my media background I had contacts with a number of really good writers. We could also take some of the investigative news service ideas I'd had and incorporate them into the magazine. Finally, I'd be able to move back to the Bay Area and live in Berkeley.

What really sold me on the idea, however, was that I truly believed we could use *Ramparts* to reach a mass audience and bring about social change. I returned to Washington, packed up a couple of things, and headed West. (While packing I committed one of the truly obnoxious acts of my life: In a fit of revolutionary cleansing, I threw my recently bought television set into the river, which was both stupid and environmentally unsound.)

I arrived in Berkeley and showed up at the *Ramparts* offices. I was ready to help lead the vanguard of the revolution that was going to change the world. Only one small problem: When I turned around to look at our followers, nobody was there . . . the Movement was over.

For a couple of months I tried to recreate the energy that made me come out West in the first place. It was hopeless. There was no potency left in the left. I should have listened to Izzy.

I. F. (Isidor Feinstein) Stone, Izzy to all of us, was a gadfly journalist who'd been covering politics since the 1920s. He was a modern day Tom Paine, oozing *Common Sense,* hammering away at tyranny, injustice, exploitation, and every other form of chicanery modern-day politicians could serve up. His *I.F. Stone Weekly* was essential reading for anyone wanting to know what duplicity and falsehoods the establishment might be selling us.

Izzy, short and plump with thick-lensed steel-rimmed glasses, could have passed as either Ben Franklin or one of the grandfathers in *Revenge of the Nerds.* Stone was a man who refused to compromise his principles for the sake of employment. Aided by his wife, and working out of their modest home on the outskirts of Washington, Izzy would do his own reporting, researching, writing, and editing and put out a quality publication that was both accurate and interesting. He answered to nobody and, with a thin, impish smile, he would describe himself as an anachronism and a most dangerous fellow with a compulsion to "cover the universe in four pages."

Izzy viewed U.S. military involvement in Vietnam as a catastrophe, which explained why we were marching together with a group of Vietnam vets in the spring of 1971.

Dewey Canyon III (Dewey Canyons I and II had taken place two years before in Southeast Asia when elements of the Third Marine Division invaded Laos) was a five-day protest in Washington, DC organized by Vietnam Veterans Against the War (VVAW). It was billed as "a limited incursion in the country of Congress."

The vets, led by senator-to-be John Kerry of Massachusetts, had received intensive media coverage throughout the week. On Friday thousands of veterans, joined by what Izzy branded "a fortuitous collection of the dissatisfied," marched to the steps of the Capitol and cast their medals and ribbons onto the steps of Congress. It was a highly emotional demonstration and I was very moved by it.

As we were standing there I turned to Izzy and said, "We're going to win! Things are going to change."

I'll never forget the sad, resigned look on his face. He took my arm and walked me over to a bench.

"Nothing's going to change," he said. "I've seen snot-nosed kids like you guys come and go. You're not going to change much."

"But . . ." I tried to protest. Izzy stopped me.

"Listen, David, it takes a lifetime to bring about social change. Your generation hasn't the patience or discipline. In fact, I don't think the species has ever produced a throng that needed such instant gratification."

"But look what's been happening this year," I protested. "Hundreds of thousands of kids came to Washington to protest the war. None of them believe that their elders are their betters. They'll— we'll change things—we really will."

"Three problems with your hypothesis," Izzy went on. "To begin with, the state is not going to just quietly melt away. You don't think that Misters Hoover, Nixon, Agnew and company haven't put together the resources to smash you down if you even get close to threatening them?"

Of course he was right. The FBI and other government agencies had already put together an impressive array of manpower to infiltrate and subvert both the radical and student left. Ironically, this thinking would lead Nixon and his people to go after not only those who actively opposed them, but also those who did not actively agree with them. The inevitable result was Watergate.

"Secondly," Izzy went on, "You kids are obsessed with violence. Maybe you all watched too many Westerns when you were kids. Too much TV."

Again, he was spot on. In the previous two years there had been over three hundred major bombings linkable to the radical left. Draft boards, induction centers, and other federal offices had been the targets. Thirty ROTC buildings were burned or bombed during the first week in May of 1972 alone. National Guard units had been mobilized on twenty-one campuses in sixteen states to deal with student disruptions.

"As the violence escalates, you'll lose the center. Soon all that will be left will be hard-core extremists . . . most of them crazy, or acting out against their parents." He sadly shook his head. "And of course that gives the state the right to retaliate in force . . . not only against the perpetrators, but against anyone who sympathizes with them as well. But that's not why your movement is going to fail." Izzy stood up and began walking back toward his car. "It's going to miscarry because you have no agenda. All any of you ever do is tell us what's wrong . . . nobody has come up with a plan to follow. There's no blueprint, no master conception of what you want." Izzy sadly shook his head. "And without that you can't change anything, because if you don't know where you're going, how can you have a strategy to get there?"

We reached his car. "Listen, the Soviet Union's leaders are the same wooden Indians as we have here, and the Chinese peasant is just as exploited as he ever was, but Marx and Mao at least had a vision. They had a program, one they could get people to risk everything to follow. What do you kids have?"

I didn't know what to say. I desperately wanted him to be wrong—but in my gut, and even worse, in my heart, I knew he was right.

I guess I looked like I was going to cry or something because Izzy put his arm around my shoulder and gave it a hug.

"Listen, all we can do is fight the good fight one day at a time," he smiled. He reached into his pocket and found a crumpled-up piece of paper. "Lillian Hellman wrote this . . . I think I'm going to run it in the monthly. She's talking about you kids. 'God knows many of them are fools and most of them will be sellouts, but they're a better generation than we were. Since when are youths not allowed to be asses?' " He squeezed my shoulder and got into his car. I think he was one of the greatest men I've ever known.

Watergate

A plumber, *as defined in Webster's New World Dictionary,*
is a skilled worker who can repair leaks. Thus it was a
misnomer for us to have labeled that inept group of burglars
who broke into the Watergate the plumbers. Richard Nixon's
men were neither skilled nor remotely capable of fixing leaks.

Their sorry path can be traced back to a Harris poll taken at
the beginning of 1972. It showed Edmund Muskie, the
Democratic senator from Maine and likely presidential
nominee, running dead even with Richard Nixon. The
Republicans were in trouble. The country was sick of the war,
worried about the economy, pissed off about busing, distressed
with its children, and terrified about the alarming rise of
violent crime. The congressional elections in 1970 had been
a Democratic landslide, giving them twelve new House seats
and eleven new governorships. It was the GOP's worst showing
since the Goldwater disaster of 1964.

The Republican brain trust blamed Nixon. John Mitchell, his attorney general and top political operative, told Nixon that during the elections he had acted like he was running for sheriff instead of for President. Something had to be done. The Republicans decided to get politics out of the White House and let Nixon appear to be above the fray. They formed the independent Citizens Committee for the Reelection of the President, aptly known as CREEP.

Money had begun to burn a hole in CREEP's moral pocket. They had collected tens of millions of dollars for the campaign. How could they best spend it to ensure the reelection of the incumbent? Enter the fertile and somewhat warped mind of G. Gordon Liddy. Liddy had recently been fired by the U.S. Treasury Department because of an extra-curricular outing at a National Rifle Association rally where he had waxed rhapsodic over gun ownership. He was hired to work as counsel for the director of security of CREEP.

Liddy was joined by another rising star within the organization. E. Howard Hunt, an ex-CIA operative and like Liddy a true believer. They began to put together a master plan for political espionage. The parapolitical stunts they thought up were awesome. They became masters of the art of politricks.

When I was a kid, my friends and I used to make up lists of who liked us and who didn't. Richard Nixon sat in the Oval

Office and did the same thing, only he called his the "enemies list." The president was a world-class hater. Paul Newman, Jack Anderson, Jane Fonda, Gregory Peck, Daniel Schorr, and Barbra Streisand all made the list. So did the head of the Otis Elevator Company. Seems the elevator at Nixon's western White House didn't work too well. Nixon unleashed the federal bureaucracy to go after his foes. The Internal Revenue Service and FBI were ordered to harass Nixon's opponents.

Meanwhile Liddy and Hunt couldn't wait to get their greedy paws on those millions in the Republican coffers. In the office of the attorney general at the Department of Justice they met with top Nixon officials and laid out a multi-million-dollar operation known as Gemstone. It included, among other gems: tapping Democrats' phones, beating the crap out of anti-Nixon demonstrators, kidnapping anti-war leaders and holding them in Mexico during the Republican convention, and leasing a yacht with hired prostitutes during the Democratic convention in Miami Beach in which the girls would pump sensitive information out of horny Democrats and photograph them in compromising positions. John Dean, the President's general counsel, called the presentation "mind-boggling." What was truly mind-boggling is that eventually a number of Liddy's plans were approved. He was given hundreds of thousands of dollars by the Commit-

tee to Reelect, and more or less carte blanche to mess with the Constitution. Fortunately for the country, he and his gang were as incompetent as they were evil.

———

Tricec Hahn Office Properties had to be the luckiest group of businessmen and women in America. The company's building, located in downtown Washington, leased a little over three hundred units and had had a one hundred percent occupancy rate for almost thirty-five years. Of course it helped that Tricec Hahn owned one of the most famous buildings in the world—it's called the Watergate.

On June 17, 1972, at around 2 A.M., the District of Columbia's "bum squad"—a group of plainclothes policemen—found Hunt and Liddy and their group of accomplices, nicely dressed in coats and ties, standing in the Watergate offices of the Democratic National Committee. They had illegally broken in and were planting bugs on the phones of the Democrats' party chairman. The Republic would never be the same.

WASHINGTON

OCTOBER 1972

Keep on Truckin' . . .
ROBERT CRUMB

One of the advantages of working as a Washington-based literary agent in the 1970s was my unlimited access to the fifth-floor news room of the *Washington Post.* A couple of times a week I would wander over and stroll across the cavernous room, stopping at various reporters' desks to gossip and plot. It seemed as if all of them wanted to write a book.

One of the dirty little secrets of American journalism in those days was that most reporters wanted out. A huge number of journalists were bored, underpaid, and tired of seeing their hard work appear on the bottoms of kitty litter boxes the next day. One prominent national reporter pleaded with me to get him a book contract so he'd be free. "You know what my job is?" he asked. "It's saying Senator Sims is dead to people who never knew Senator Sims was ever alive."

Almost all the journalists felt they had a book in them, and in those days I didn't realize that that was an excellent place to keep it. Anyway, I think it amused Ben Bradlee, managing editor of the *Post,* to see the feeding frenzy my presence on the fifth floor caused.

One reporter who was hot to do a book was Carl Bernstein, a former copyboy for the *Washington Star* (the now defunct afternoon paper). He had become a full-time reporter at nineteen and had already been at the *Post* for six years. Carl's intelligence was matched only by his indolence. He was the kind of guy whose teachers probably sent home notes reading: "Carl is so bright and special. How do we get him to sit still, pay attention, and do his work?" The editors at the *Post* had the same problem with him. They didn't know whether they should promote Carl or fire him.

We'd met the year before. I liked Carl instantly. He had an attitude. Always one of the sloppiest guys in the newsroom, with long, unruly hair down to his shoulders, Carl was the embodiment of adult attention deficit disorder. He was the only guy who could fall asleep in the newsroom and get away with it.

Carl and I had gotten very excited about his doing a book called *The Hope Business.* It was meant to be an investigative look into the various businesses that preyed upon the hopes and aspirations of people who wanted to better themselves. He'd look at everything from the company that put out the matchbook covers stating, "We're looking for people who like to draw" to dating services for the elderly. It was to be like a series of *60 Minutes* pieces in a book format. I interested a number of publishers in the project and Carl was supposed to write up a short proposal. The problem was, Carl forgot to write the proposal. Something always came up: He'd met a new woman, he'd not been feeling well, he'd had to go out of town on assignment. Fortunately, I don't believe Carl owned a dog at the time or I'm sure I would have heard about the canine accidentally chomping Carl's proposal.

When Carl finally called I figured I'd hear another series of excuses about *The Hope Business,* but instead he told me he had an idea for another book, a story he and his new partner, some guy named Bob Woodward, were working on. "Think anyone would buy a book about Watergate?" he asked.

Martha reached across the bed for John, but he wasn't there.
The Attorney General was on the phone with the Western White
house. There was a problem.

So began Bernstein and Woodward's book proposal about how a
group of idiots (the plumbers) had tried to subvert the Constitution
at the behest of the Nixon government.

We wrote the proposal at Woodward's apartment, and I thought
it was pretty damn good. So what if Watergate had not been in the
news for a while? So what if Nixon looked like he was going to be
overwhelmingly reelected in a few weeks? I still thought it was a
solid piece of work that publishers would snap up.

Woodward and Bernstein—although in those days they were
referred to as Bernstein and Woodward—were anxious to get a
quick sale. Neither was making much at the *Post*. Woodward was
making about three hundred dollars a week. More importantly, the
rest of the national press had more or less ignored their work. In
the fall of 1972 most major papers had not yet assigned full-time
coverage to Watergate, and Carl and Bob felt both underexposed
and unappreciated. A big book would take care of that.

One of the best ways of getting a quick sale on a book is to auction it. I told the boys I was going to offer the book proposal simultaneously to ten publishers. I made ten copies of their treatment and
sent it out to publishers. I purposely did not send it to Simon &
Schuster. I felt I had enough books in their basket, and anyway, I
wanted to establish relationships with other houses. Bids were supposed to come in on Monday. A watched phone never rings. Not one
call—except from Carl and Bob, who called every five minutes to
find out what was happening. Finally I began calling the publishers.

"Just a third-rate burglary, not really a book," said the editor in
chief of a major house. I tried arguing that the story might have
wider implications, but he wasn't interested.

"Washington books don't sell. Anyway, we've got enough political stuff on our list," said another.

"Nixon's going to be reelected in a landslide and we don't want any trouble." I called the guy a chickenshit liberal and hung up.

Ten passes, not even a nibble. I swallowed my pride and called my best friend and mentor, Dick Snyder, president of Simon & Schuster, and asked for a meeting. As luck would have it, he was going to be in Washington the next morning.

I called Carl and Bob and gave them the bad news about our auction. They were not pleased. "Don't panic," I told them. "It's going to be okay. Be at the Hay Adams Hotel at ten o'clock tomorrow morning. We're going to meet with the president of Simon & Schuster. I guarantee he'll buy it."

I was calling them from New York, where I'd gone in case any of the bidders wanted to meet. Suddenly, I had a lot of free time.

———

I stayed with the late Jerry Rubin at his apartment in the Village. Tom Forcade, founder and editor of *High Times* Magazine, and a true madman, came by to pick me up and take me to A. J. Weberman's house. Weberman was a garbologist; he collected famous people's trash and made collages out of it. He'd just gotten Henry Kissinger's garbage and wanted to show it to us.

We went to A. J.'s place and pored over Henry's trash for awhile. I'd always found Weberman an interesting character. On Bob Dylan's thirtieth birthday, A. J. presented him with a birthday cake with thirty hypodermic needles in it because Dylan had gone electric.

Tom Forcade, as one would expect from the founder of *High Times,* was not a fellow who spent many evenings sober. (A couple of years later Tom put a gun to his head and shot what was left of his brains out. To paraphrase Noel Coward, he must have been a marvelous shot.) He'd been bringing us drinks all evening. As he handed us our refills, he announced, "By the way, this is some of the best acid I've ever scored." I spit my drink out, jumped to my feet, and made a grab for Tom, who neatly ducked behind A. J.

"Oh, I put tabs of acid in each of your drinks. Have a nice trip," Tom gleefully told us. I rushed back to Jerry's, but I knew that was not going to be a safe haven. I jumped in a cab and went to the old Americana Hotel. I'd stayed there as a kid when my dad took us to the 1960 World's Fair.

This was not happening. I had the most important meeting of my life the next day. I picked up the phone, "Operator, listen— you've got to have someone call me tomorrow and remind me to take the seven o'clock shuttle to Washington. Huh? This is the fourth time I've called to tell you that? No, you don't have to send up security. I won't call again." I was in big trouble.

Somehow I made it to Washington the next morning. Most of the people on my flight kept morphing into barnyard animals, but, hey, what could I do?

I got to the hotel just as Carl and Bob were arriving. They were both wrecks. That morning they'd broken a story that was completely wrong. Ben Bradlee was really pissed and the two boys were in a panic. Dick, meanwhile, was in a foul mood. He never liked being away from home and he had a horrible night's sleep. I sat in the corner trying to come down. The meeting was a disaster.

Finally, Carl and Bob left. Dick began packing his things and shook his head. "Pass," he said. Maybe it was crashing from the LSD. Maybe it was some kind of spiritual missive being sent by a higher power. I don't know what happened, but I did something I'd never done before or since in a meeting. I began to cry. Not just crying, but pitiful weeping.

Dick Snyder is not the kind of man who is known for a keen sense of humanity, but I think this truly unnerved him. I bawled, "You got to buy this book or I can never do business with you again." He stared at me openmouthed. "Please, Dick—sob, gulp—please."

Dick slowly walked up to me and grabbed my shoulder. I wasn't sure if he was going to slap me or hug me. He took a deep breath, looked me in the eye, and nodded his head. "David, I've never seen anyone care so much about a book. I'll buy it." The rest, as they say, is history.

WASHINGTON

We can't all be heroes because somebody has to sit
on the curb and clap as they go by . . .
WILL ROGERS

For the next half year we all anxiously awaited a first draft of the book, but the boys were stuck. The Watergate story continued to unfold. Where should they cut it off? What was the real story? Was the president involved?

Simon & Schuster got antsy. A couple of times they mentioned that maybe it might be a good idea to return the advance.

In the early spring of 1973, however, the Watergate cover-up began to unravel. James McCord, one of the men convicted of the break-in, sent a note to Judge Sirica, the man who was to sentence him. He told the judge that there was a lot he and the others hadn't mentioned during the trial and he'd be obliged to tell it all if the judge would give him an audience—oh, and was there any possibility that if he told the truth this time he wouldn't have to go to prison for the next thirty years?

Like extras fleeing the *Titanic,* Nixon's men began to jump ship. Carl and Bob were right in the middle of reporting it. The book would have to wait.

The boys were far ahead of the rest of the newspaper business in ferreting out the Watergate story. Only one other reporter gave them any competition—my old friend Sy Hersh.

At the height of the Watergate scandal, Sy had been working for the *New York Times* for almost a year. He'd broken a number of top stories and was regarded as the fair-haired boy of the newsroom. When his editors first asked him to cover Watergate, Sy was somewhat reluctant. His best sources were not in the executive branch of government, and investigative reporters are not any better than their sources. Also, he'd have to play some serious catch-up. The *Post* had been on the story since the break-in. Carl and Bob (well, at least Bob) worked as hard as Sy and seemed to have a front-page story in the paper each week.

Sy, a fiercely competitive human being, couldn't stand being beaten either on the tennis court or at the newsstand, so he accepted the challenge. It was too good a story to miss.

Within a few months Hersh and the *Times* were not only matching the boys but beating them on a number of Watergate stories. Good news for the country, but bad news for me.

———

The phone rang at seven in the morning. I was still fast asleep. It was Bernstein. "You tell your friend Hersh he's going the wrong way on the Dean story." I struggled to gain some semblance of consciousness. I'm a night person and being up this early was cruel and unusual.

A couple of days later it happened again—at 6:30 in the morning—only it was Hersh this time. "Tell your pals Bernstein and Woodward that Mardian is *not, NOT* to be trusted. . . . You hear me?" I tried to write it down and knocked over a glass of juice.

These early morning calls went on for months. I somehow became a go-between for the best investigative reporters in the country, which, don't get me wrong, was fun and exciting. But it seriously cut into my God-given right to a few hours of sleep each night.

For a while I considered taking the phone off the hook before I went to bed, but I decided against it. Carl and Bob were my clients. Sy was one of my best friends. I tried to go to bed earlier, but it was no use. My body clock was set for evening. I couldn't fall asleep. It was useless to ask them to stop calling me. These were three very driven men.

I pleaded with Carl and Bob to let me set up a meeting with Sy so that the three of them could get to know each other and not have to use me as a go-between. Bernstein and Woodward finally agreed to meet, but stipulated that it must be some place very, very private. Elated, I went to Sy's office to set it up. Sy shook his head. "No, bad idea. I think we'll all do a better job if we remain at arm's length." I begged him to just have lunch with the guys. Sy got angry. "What do you think would happen to us if Nixon got a picture of Bernstein, Woodward, and Hersh sitting together?" He pounded the table. "He'd claim we were all part of some fucking press conspiracy. He'd use it against us every time we broke a story." He snarled, "I'm not meeting with them. Period!"

After a couple of months I was up first thing in the morning even when they didn't call. It was the anticipation of the phone ringing that now awakened me. I looked horrible, big bags under my eyes. I had no energy. I couldn't wait for Watergate to end.

Around the third month of this torture I got a call from Sy. He told me I was right, that I shouldn't have to be a conduit. "Let's have dinner tonight," he said.

I was thrilled! I tracked down Carl and Bob and they agreed to dinner. Yes! I arranged for us to meet at a Chinese restaurant far out on the Robert E. Lee Highway in Virginia.

Watching the boys and Sy talk for the first time was like watching the world series of poker. Carl put a piece of information about Watergate on the table and Sy quickly topped it. Carl, upon hearing Sy's info, raised it by a source. Bob looked at Carl with that "are you crazy telling him that" look and Carl, I think just to piss Bob off, would tell even more.

I witnessed Nixon's worst nightmare: the *New York Times* and the *Washington Post* breaking bread (actually fortune cookies) together and sharing information about the Watergate conspiracy.

After dinner Sy suggested that we go over to the house of a reporter we all knew for a drink. The boys gladly accepted and the evening continued.

As I drove back to Washington I was amazed at how well everything had gone. What astounded me most, however, was that Sy wanted to have a drink with the guys.

Sy is an extremely private person. Sometimes he and his wife Liz had family or friends of their kids over for dinner, but that was it. As a rule he didn't go to parties, he didn't go to dinners, and he certainly didn't go out drinking with the boys. My antennae tingled.

The reporter was happy to see us. He invited us in and poured us drinks. We sat in the living room and continued to talk. Actually, it was more like we were gossiping at an extraordinary high level.

We were onto our second beers when Bob left to go to the bathroom. A moment later he stormed into the living room and headed for the door. He turned to Carl and shouted, "Let's go." Carl, as confused as I was, didn't move. Bob got a look on his face that Carl obviously had seen before and he jumped up from the couch. Before he could thank Sy for the evening, Bob pushed him out the door.

Sy sat there for a minute, then laughed. "He must have used the phone in the kitchen to call his desk," he said. Sy was laughing hard. I'd never seen him so happy.

"What is it? What's going on?" I demanded.

Sy couldn't control himself. He actually fell off the couch.

"Read tomorrow's paper," he gasped. "I popped a big one."

Bob must have called the *Post*'s desk to see what was happening and gotten the riot act read to him.

See, every evening the *Post* and the *Times* get a copy of the front page of each other's first edition. This is not just a courtesy, but an insurance policy. If the *Times* had a big story on the front page and the *Post* didn't have it, the *Post* had a chance to put a reporter on the piece and match it for the home delivery edition, and vice versa.

"A Watergate piece?" I asked, suddenly beginning to understand.

"Yeah, I got a piece about Richard Kleindienst. Nixon's attorney general is in big trouble. It's the lead story in the *Times*, and the *Post* is going to have to use my story because they couldn't find Bernstein and Woodward to match it!" Sy gleefully proclaimed. He had sandbagged the boys.

The next morning my bedside clock read 6:00 A.M. when the phone rang. I picked it up. "You tell your friend Hersh he's a goddamn . . ."

WASHINGTON

But he hasn't got any clothes on . . .
THE EMPEROR'S NEW CLOTHES

There is nothing covered, that shall not be revealed;
neither hid, that shall not be known . . .
KING JAMES BIBLE

As Woodward and Bernstein's agent I had once again become a celebrity by association. Like most people, I enjoyed being the center of attention. Actually, I'd become addicted to it. And now I had something other than My Lai and Ellsberg to talk about.

All the President's Men was another fix of fame. Everyone wanted to talk about Watergate and the boys. The two most frequently asked questions were: (1) Did you guys make a ton of money? (2) Who was Deep Throat?

The answer to (1) is that it's nobody's business but God's and the IRS's. Yes, *All the President's Men* and the boys' follow-up book, *The Final Days,* sold in excess of half a million hardcover copies. Both books had seven-figure paperback sales and big foreign rights sales, and the boys were paid huge advances for the dramatic rights.

The answer to (2) is a little more complicated.

Like millions of others, I greatly admired the job Carl Bernstein and Bob Woodward did in pursuing the truth about Richard Nixon and his advisors in both the Watergate break-in and its subsequent cover-up. The fact that they were able to help prove that

Nixon and his followers broke the rules of fair play in a democratic society is one of the great success stories in American journalism. My problem with Carl and Bob, though, is how their tale was told.

In the original proposal of *All the President's Men*, Deep Throat did not exist. When I got an early copy of the rough first draft of the book I was fascinated by this new character. Was he real? I was both thrilled at how exciting a read the book had become and apprehensive about the addition of the new personality to the historical mix. Who was this guy Deep Throat? Like others, I had my doubts about whether or not he actually existed. Nobody at the *Post* or at Simon & Schuster had ever mentioned him.

Bob Fink, a brilliant researcher, had been hired by Bob and Carl to work on the book. His tireless research and organizational skills had enabled the boys to get *All the President's Men* in manuscript form. Fink, too, had no idea where the character of Deep Throat had come from and was equally surprised to see him as such an integral part of the book.

I decided that Deep Throat must be a composite. I called Sy Hersh, whose judgment as an investigative journalist I trusted, and asked if it was kosher to combine various sources into a composite character. Sy gave me an emphatic no. I discussed the question with a number of other people and got mixed reactions. But, hey, this was Woodward and Bernstein. They had to know what they were doing. So the book was published as it was, and the motion picture came out shortly thereafter.

In early April 1976 I attended a benefit premiere of the movie version of *All the President's Men* at the Kennedy Center in Washington, DC. It was like a scene out of *Day of the Locust*. That month the *Post* was involved in a bitter strike with its pressmen. On one side of the entrance to the theater were the pressmen chanting slogans and singing "We Shall Overcome." On the other side were thousands of fans acting like it was Academy Award night. The crowd screamed wildly as Dustin Hoffman, Woodward and Bernstein, Jason Robards, Martin Balsam, and the other stars of the movie arrived. When the producer and star of the feature, Robert Redford, showed up, they went nuts.

So did Redford. I was in the men's room when he walked in and spotted me. We'd met a number of times before. I liked Redford. He was smart, he had strong convictions about his work, and, of course, he was a movie star.

Instead of receiving a firm handshake from Bob, I found myself slammed up against the bathroom wall. I don't know what there is about me that makes people want to slam me against walls.

"You've ruined my goddamn life!" he growled.

"How?" I gasped.

"By releasing *The Final Days* early!"

Bernstein and Woodward's sequel was supposed to come out after the opening of *All the President's Men*, but we had to move our publication date up a few weeks when columnist Liz Smith began publishing parts of the book in her column. Liz had gotten the book from one of my authors, Kitty Kelley. Because of deadline problems, Kitty couldn't get it into her own publication, *New Times*, so instead she leaked it to her buddy Liz. How Kitty got the book is still unknown, but I had nothing to do with giving it to her. Still, there was a trail of circumstantial evidence pointing toward me. As agent and owner of ten percent of the profits of the book, I'd be shooting myself in the pocketbook by leaking it. I guess that never occurred to Redford.

"This is going to kill the movie. Everyone's going to be feeling sorry for Nixon now. You've screwed me!" Redford yelled.

In fact, the book built enormous interest in the movie. The very first nonfiction book ever to go onto the *New York Times* bestseller list as number one in its debut week, it stayed there twenty more weeks. The movie, too, was a huge success. On its first weekend it set attendance records in almost every theater. It made almost seventy million dollars (in 1976 dollars) and was the second highest grossing film of the year. (*Rocky* was number one.) *All the President's Men* made everyone's best of the year list and was nominated for eight Academy Awards.

Of course, Redford didn't know any of this was going to happen when he held me against the wall in the men's room at the Kennedy Center. To him, I'd wiped out a year's worth of hard work.

"Well, what do you have to say for yourself?" he said, putting his amazingly handsome face next to mine. "You ruined my career!"

"Um," I mumbled. "Bob, I promise I'll never do it again."

I went back to my seat feeling terrible. But that was nothing compared to how I felt as I watched the movie for the first time.

The poster advertising the movie claimed it was "The Most Devastating Detective Story of This Century." It was, but for the wrong reasons. Carl and Bob had suddenly become larger-than-life characters who had risked their very being to bring the American people the truth about Watergate. There was only one problem with this wonderful account. It wasn't true. At one point in the movie, Deep Throat tells Bob Woodward that his life is in danger. *There they go again,* I thought. When I first read the book I was shocked that Bob wrote about how their lives were in peril. Of course their professional careers had been at risk. But their personal safety? In danger from whom? Nixon's guys? Yes, the president and all his men may have hated Woodward and Bernstein's guts—they said so publicly a number of times. Nixon was even caught on tape that spring whining that Woodward and Bernstein had better watch their "damn cotton-picking faces." But Nixon's people couldn't even pull off a third-rate burglary. How could they ever arrange a hit on two high-profile reporters with the whole world watching?

How could Deep Throat tell them such a thing? I sat there feeling very uncomfortable. What was going on? Then I remembered Deep Throat's earlier admonition to Bob: "Follow the money . . ." Interestingly enough, that line is not to be found in the book version of *All the President's Men*. Perhaps Bob only remembered Deep Throat's words after he received three hundred fifty thousand dollars from Warner Brothers.

When we first sold the book to Simon & Schuster, it was called *Reporting Watergate*, an insider's account of what had happened. It was meant to be similar to Theodore White's *Making of the President* series, which was so popular at that time. All this changed when Robert Redford entered the creative equation.

Redford had just finished making *The Candidate*, an Oscar-winning story about an idealist who tries to maintain his integrity while seeking a seat in the United States Senate. Redford had gotten a taste for politics and was fascinated by the dynamics of Watergate. Furthermore, he was enthralled with the relationship between the off-the-wall Jewish dropout Bernstein and the ice-cold WASP Yalie Woodward. He sensed a great movie.

Redford invited Woodward to a dinner party hosted by Jack Valenti where he introduced Woodward to William Goldman, a wonderful screenwriter who had written *Butch Cassidy and the Sundance Kid*. The three of them began to talk about turning Carl and Bob's story into a movie. Woodward told the two men about the book he was working on and they strongly urged him to change the tone of the work from a general overview of the Watergate crisis to a blow-by-blow account of the boys' personal involvement. Woodward loved the idea and soon convinced Carl that this was the right tack for the book. This may have been how Deep Throat was conceived.

Without Deep Throat in *All the President's Men*, there's no book or movie. After Redford and Hoffman, he is the most important character in the film. The ultimate aim of any writer is to create a character that is real, alive, and believable. Deep Throat satisfies all those criteria in the book and movie—but what about in real life?

One of my biggest problems with Deep Throat was the physical evidence presented in the book. Woodward says that when he had an urgent inquiry to make of Deep Throat, he would move an old flowerpot to the rear of his balcony. He'd put a stick with a one-foot square red cloth attached into the pot as his signal to Deep Throat to meet. I guess Deep Throat was supposed to drive by Woodward's apartment daily to see if the pot was on the balcony; if so, they would meet at 2:00 A.M. in a prearranged underground parking garage.

Very romantic, but it does raise a couple of questions. The first is the unlikeliness that anyone as important as Deep Throat was supposed to have been would take time off each day for a leisurely drive over to Bob's to see if the old flowerpot was out. Second, I'd been to Bob's apartment. It didn't face the street, it faced an alley. If Deep Throat wanted to see if a meeting was on, he would have had to get out of his car and enter a small courtyard, then crane his neck to see if the flowerpot on Bob's sixth-floor balcony was out. I couldn't imagine a high government official, especially one who doesn't want to be linked to Woodward and the *Post*, risking hanging out in Woodward's courtyard every night to see if Bob wanted to meet.

Further, Bob claimed that if Deep Throat wanted to meet him, he would allegedly mark page 20 of Woodward's *New York Times* with the hands of a clock indicating the time of the requested rendezvous. But Bob got his paper in the front lobby of his building. The papers were unmarked and stacked in a pile. How did Deep Throat know which one was Bob's? Moreover, how did Deep Throat get a hold of Woodward's paper? The front door to his building was locked. Did Woodward give him a key so he could come into the lobby and mark his paper? In the book Bob says that the *Times* was delivered to his building before seven o'clock each morning, so poor Deep Throat would have to wait in the early hours outside Bob's apartment for the *Times* delivery man to arrive, politely ask him if he could borrow a paper, mark page 20 with his clock, put the paper back in the pile, and hope that Woodward would instinctively pick the marked paper.

The flowerpot and newspaper scenes work well in both the book and movie. They bring cloak-and-dagger drama to the account. I think the creative team for the book and movie faced a dilemma—how do you make the narrative flow of Woodward and Bernstein's story exciting? How do you get around the problem of countless talking heads exchanging information? The solution, of course, is Deep Throat.

Another problem I had with Deep Throat was that so much of what he told Woodward was wrong. For example, Deep Throat says that Senator Howard Baker of Tennessee, the ranking Republican member of the Senate Watergate committee, is "in the bag and reporting directly back to the White House." Pure nonsense. In fact, Nixon was incensed that he couldn't get Baker to cooperate and give his staff inside information. He was caught on tape calling Baker a "simpering asshole." On the same day he exploded and told White House congressional liaison William Timmons, "Now Howard Baker ... will never be in the White House again—never, never, never. The softballs he threw up to Dean. What he did to John Mitchell was unforgivable. He's finished." Hardly the way one would describe a man who was completely in the bag.

Deep Throat tells Woodward that Nixon threatened Dean personally and that if he ever revealed anything the president would ensure he went to jail. Never happened. When I was John Dean's agent I asked him about this and he told me that the President never would have had a direct confrontation with him, that Nixon never did any of his dirty work face to face. That's why he had Haldeman and Ehrlichman around. One more of Deep Throat's facts was patently fiction. Deep Throat warns Woodward that the cover-up has little to do with Watergate, that it is mainly to protect covert operations of the United States intelligence community. He goes on to tell Bob that the CIA is deeply involved. Wrong again. In fact, the June 23 1972 smoking gun tape that finally brought Nixon down is about the White House conspiring to call CIA director Richard Helms and his deputy General Vernon Walters and direct them to get the FBI to call off the investigation because it would impinge on CIA operations. Helms and Walters refused to do so and told Nixon that the CIA didn't want anything to do with Watergate. And Woodward couldn't have known that because the tapes had not yet been released. Once again, it was likely that Deep Throat's inside information was pure rubbish.

At the end of *All the President's Men,* Bob breathlessly rushes to Carl and types "Everyone's life is in danger. Electronic surveillance is going on and we'd better watch it."

"Who is doing it?" Bernstein asks.

"The C-I-A," Woodward answers.

How many kids who watched the movie went on to believe that our major intelligence service was in the business of trying to assassinate reporters? None of this was true. The *Washington Post* did sweep its newsroom for bugs, but after spending in excess of five thousand dollars found nothing. Finally, The *Washington Post* Corporation was, at the time of the Watergate stories, worth hundreds of millions of dollars. Bob Woodward was not yet thirty years old and he had been working at the *Post* for less than a year. It is hard to believe that the *Post* would have risked its financial future on the word of a rookie reporter's anonymous source. The *Post* took on the most powerful men in the United States. They couldn't afford to be wrong.

The list of misinformation goes on and on. My purpose is not to rewrite the history of the Watergate investigation; there are well over two hundred books already on that subject. My intention is simply to point out the many inconsistencies we find in the so-called existence of Deep Throat. When I contacted Carl and Bob to tell them my allegations, both vehemently denied them and claimed that Deep Throat is, in fact, a real person whose identity they will reveal after he dies. In addition, Woodward said that he thinks I'm an asshole.

Bob and Carl clearly had fantastic sources who, for a variety of reasons, were willing to take great risks to leak information to the *Washington Post*. That Bob and Carl would protect such sources is admirable. That they would combine their sources into a composite character is both clever and creative. That the American public would believe them is understandable. The basic concern regarding Deep Throat, however, is best stated by Friedreich Nietzsche, who warned us that those who fight monsters should see to it that in the process they do not become monsters themselves.

It's now more than twenty-five years since Bob Woodward and Deep Throat allegedly first met in the shadowy confines of a subterranean parking garage in the nation's capital. Their enemies have long since passed from the scene. Yet Deep Throat has still not come forward to be hailed as a great American hero. He can't, because he does not exist.

Actually he does, and in the opening credits of *All the President's Men* we're told exactly who he is: Deep Throat is Hal Holbrook.

Publishing

Former governor James Earl "Jimmy" Carter of Georgia had one thing going for him in the 1976 presidential elections— he wasn't Gerald Ford. A political neophyte, he won a clear-cut mandate from the country to throw the Republican "crooks" out. "I'll never tell you a lie," he promised the electorate, and they believed him. Carter was the first southern president since Zachary Taylor (1849–1850), and his "born again" energy and fervor were balm to a nation rubbed raw by the turmoil of the Nixon scandals.

The five-billion-dollar Metro subway finally opened in Washington, DC, but people were afraid to ride it because of President Ford's warning about the coming epidemic of the swine flu. On the advice of medical authorities Ford spent over a hundred million dollars setting up an inoculation program. It was the fourth grade again for me as I stood in line to get my shot. It hurt, and I was as pissed as the rest of

the country when we found out it was all a false alarm.
Only six cases of the flu were recorded, but hundreds of those
inoculated developed Guillaume-Barre Syndrome, a rare
paralytic affliction caused by the shots. The government
got sued for billions.

Eleven million CB (citizens band) radios were sold,
creating an instant three billion dollars for the GNP and
countless hours of yakking on the byways of America. The
fax machine moved into the American business, and two
amateur electronics enthusiasts developed a computer in
their California garage and called it an Apple.

Roots, The Hite Report: A Nationwide Study of Female
Sexuality, 1876, Lyndon Johnson and the American Dream,
and The Boys from Brazil *headed the bestseller list.*

The Front, Network, Rocky, Marathon Man, Taxi Driver,
and The Man Who Fell to Earth *were notable movies of the*
year. And the pop music charts included hits by Fleetwood
Mac, Peter Frampton, Bruce Springsteen, and the Eagles.
In addition, punk rock began to creep into America at rock
clubs such as Max's Kansas City.

On the small screen, Mary Hartman, Mary Hartman;
Happy Days; Laverne and Shirley; Upstairs, Downstairs;
and Charlie's Angels *made us laugh, the miniseries*
Rich Man, Poor Man *captivated us, and NBC's* Saturday
Night Live *with John Belushi, Bill Murray, Dan Ackroyd,*

*Gilda Radner, and Chevy Chase made us all get home
by 11:30.*

*The Vietnam War was finally over. More than forty-seven
thousand American troops were killed, three hundred thousand
were wounded, and one hundred ten billion dollars of our
national treasury was spent before the last soldiers departed
in Spring 1973. Within a short time the National Liberation
Front forces had pushed southward and captured Saigon.
During thirty years of war the Vietnamese had lost over two
million dead and seen another four million wounded. Over
half of the population had been left homeless, and much of the
cultivated land and infrastructure of Vietnam was destroyed.*

*The dominos did not fall. World communism did not take
over America. We'd been right, the grown-ups wrong, but so
what? The war had sapped our national spirit. It had pushed
our generation to the very edge of the political landscape.
Our excesses had scared and repelled the body politic. The
direct result was the Reagan-Bush counterrevolution. We
would not see another Democrat in the White House until
Bill Clinton's election in the nineties.*

*But we'd achieved closure. The war was over and Nixon was
gone, accused and convicted in the public mind of "high
crimes and misdemeanors" against the state and almost
impeached for misusing the government against its own
citizens.*

It was time for us to stop trying to destroy the system and become part of it. As the Me Decade spilled into our bicentennial year, it was time for baby boomers to face the unlikely but unavoidable fact: We were about to become the grown-ups.

NEW YORK

MARCH 1976

*Under conditions of tyranny it is far easier to act
than to think . . .*
HANNAH ARENDT

I was amazed that Leni Reifenstahl was still alive, let alone holding for me on line one. Of course I knew who she was. Her Nazi
propaganda classic, *Triumph of the Will,* had blown me away when
I'd first seen it at Berkeley. Those beautiful Aryan kids looked
like they were having such a great time at Nuremberg. Who
wouldn't want to join a fun organization like the Nazis?

With the success of the Watergate books I became a full-time
literary agent. I moved to New York and actually had an office.
Well, I didn't really have an office: Jann Wenner, the founder and
head man at *Rolling Stone,* had asked me to represent the magazine on a couple of book deals. He couldn't stand not being able to
find me, so he set me up in the back of their offices.

I knew better than to ignore Ms. Reifenstahl's call. Two years
before, I'd taken a call from a polite young women who had
informed me that she was Julie Nixon Eisenhower. She asked me
if I would be interested in representing her and David on a couple
of books they wanted to write. I laughed and hung up.

Except it was really her. A couple of minutes later the writer
Ben Stein (currently the star of *Win Ben Stein's Money*) called in a
panic.

"How could you do that!" he yelled. "I recommended you to David and Julie and you hung up on them?" Oops. I quickly got their number from Ben, apologized profusely, and called them back.

In the interests of full disclosure, I told Julie that I'd spent most of my adult life trying to bring down her father, but she wanted me to represent them anyway. She and David had heard that I was fair, fun, and fearless. (I immediately wanted to have new business cards printed and use that as my logo.) I arranged to meet them in Washington, found the two of them to be quite serious about doing books, and quickly found publishers for both projects (*Special People* and *Eisenhower*).

I grew to like David and Julie immensely. They were polite, caring, generous, warm-hearted people. I found it impossible to reconcile their existence with the monster I perceived Julie's father to be. In fact, if I had been forced to let any of the Watergate principals raise my son Oly, I would have picked David and Julie.

I picked up line one. Ms. Reifenstahl wanted to write a book and needed a publisher. I took her number and said that I'd call her back.

That afternoon I did a bit of research into her life. I discovered that she was basically Hitler's official filmmaker. After the war she'd been imprisoned as a Nazi sympathizer. Thereafter, she'd gone off to Africa and shot a series of amazing pictures that had been published in various folios. She also had become an accomplished underwater photographer and had published a number of lavish coffee table books. Now she wanted to write her memoirs.

I casually mentioned the book to a couple of editors I met with later that day. They were appalled. "She's a war criminal!" one of them thundered. "*Triumph of the Will* was one of the best recruiting tools the Third Reich had. How can you even think about working with someone like that?"

The other editor was equally sickened. "She's dirt," he said. "They shouldn't have just shaved off her hair when they put her in jail after the war. They should have shaved off her soul." He stared intently at me. "You do this book and a lot of people in this town will never work with you again."

I called Ms. Riefenstahl back and asked her if she was free for dinner.

We met at an upscale midtown restaurant. Leni was sitting at the table, indistinguishable from any of the other well-coifed, beautifully jeweled elderly women in the room. Truman Capote would have easily table-hopped to sit with her. She was still a very attractive woman. I remembered a *Time* cover I'd seen. Posing in shorts and an adorable climbing outfit, Leni had been the magazine's first cheesecake photo.

Our conversation began with that peculiar awkwardness that two strangers from diverse cultures often encounter, but soon we found a common ground for discussion: fish.

Leni Riefenstahl had a passion for deep-sea diving. I liked to snorkel. We began to trade stories. I told her about once seeing a manta ray. She told me about being trapped in a ring of deadly jellyfish. I told her about once seeing a small shark from the shore. She told me about riding the dorsal fin of a great white off Tahiti. It was clear nobody was going to one-up this woman.

Leni began to lay out her book. Her life had been fascinating indeed. She'd lived three or four completely different existences in her seventy-plus years.

I don't normally drink. I just never enjoyed the taste of it. Good wine is wasted on me. Tonight, however, we were well into our third bottle. I figured it was a European thing, so I kept on chugging to keep up with her. As a result I was soon a bit tipsy. That's probably what gave me the courage to ask her. I finished my glass, looked intently across the table and popped the big question.

"Okay, Leni—what was he really like?"

She looked back at me, not at all surprised. I'm sure she'd had to discuss her relationship with the Führer all her life. There had been persistent rumors as early as the mid-1930s that Hitler had taken Leni as a mistress. I wanted to find out how she was going to deal with this in her book. Actually, that's not really true: I really just wanted to know what he was like. I mean, how many times do you meet someone who used to associate with Adolf Hitler?

"He was great." She finished her own wine and smiled. "He'd call me up in the middle of the night and have me come over to talk with him. He'd keep me spellbound." She nodded her head. "He was the most charismatic man I've ever met. His energy and enthusiasm was breathtaking. Each time I left him . . . I'd be exhausted."

All I could do was nod my own head. So, Hitler had been a great guy to hang with.

She went on. "But Goebbels . . . he was a bad man."

I thought to myself, yes, that's probably a fair assessment of one of the Third Reich's most repugnant characters.

"A pig. I needed six cameras to shoot my movie, *Olympia* [the story of the 1936 Olympic games held in Berlin], and he'd only give me four."

"Oh," I answered. Perhaps I had been thinking of him in a slightly different historical context.

We finished dinner and stood at the restaurant's exit. Leni took my hand and held it for a long time. She had been a captivating dinner companion. Her strength of conviction and sense of excitement about her life had been moving.

"Thank you for meeting with me," she said. "I was afraid that Americans would not want to have anything to do with me."

I awkwardly mumbled something back to her. I'd really had way too much to drink, and watched as she left to get into a waiting cab. It had been a fascinating evening, but I knew now that I wouldn't do her book.

I walked out into the night and began to shiver. Maybe it was the cold night air? I was a California weather wimp. No, it was my hand. I shivered again. I stared at my hand, a hand that had just held another that forty years before had perhaps pleasured Adolf Hitler.

NEW YORK

> *The absurd is the essential concept*
> *and the first truth . . .*
> ALBERT CAMUS

I'd more or less committed full time to the book business and was having a blast. *Newsweek* had decided I was the hottest thing in books and did a feature on me called "Agent for Disaster":

> *If the nation has a trauma, it's a good bet that hustling young literary agent David Obst has 10 percent of it. A 28-year-old walking advertisement for radical cheek.*
>
> *Obst has turned Watergate into a personal gold mine . . . Not bad for a kid from Culver City. "It isn't easy being a functional illiterate and a literary agent." says Obst.*
>
> *Obst's unorthodox working habits drive his authors crazy. He disappears for days at a time, to see the comet Kohoutek in Peru or to play backgammon with Hugh Hefner and he has never answered one piece of correspondence. Woodward and Bernstein threatened to fire him unless he hired a secretary. Obst compromised by hiring an answering service.*
>
> *Today Obst's cigars are longer than his hair, and he admits that hobnobbing with publishing fat cats has tended to deradicalize him. Still, Obst gives large chunks of money away and is always ready to help an author whose book he believes in. My consciousness has been altered," says Obst, adding "I've*

258

made a good living and a good reputation from national
tragedies and I think that I'm far from out of business."

To say that I was an unorthodox literary agent would be a fair
statement. I hadn't planned on going into the book business (or
any other). I had a style that was perfectly matched to the period,
that is, I didn't take it all that seriously and had a flair for the
absurd. For example, one day when I was in San Francisco to meet
with some writers, I saw a very drunk McDonald's executive wearing a company blazer in a restaurant. The blazer was a beautiful
navy blue with the golden arches embroidered in bright yellow
over the breast pocket. I went up to the man and said, "How much
do you want for your coat?" I took out a roll of ten-dollar bills and
started peeling them off. After I got about eight or nine of them
down he took off his blazer and gave it to me. I wore that coat with
an American flag tie and tennis shoes to every important meeting
I ever went to.

I had developed an impressive roster of authors to represent,
including Bernstein and Woodward, Brit Hume, Jules Witcover,
Stanley Karnow, David and Julie Eisenhower, Jane and Michael
Stern, David Wallechinsky, Kitty Kelley, Marvel Comics, Rolling
Stone Magazine, Uri Geller, Bill Russell, Tammy Wynette, John
Dean, Taylor Branch, John Rothchild, and many, many others.

One of the great truisms of American business is that success
begets success. For the next couple of years I could do no wrong
in the book business. Authors would flock to me because I was
getting huge advances; publishers would court me because I had
important writers.

Things were coming almost too easily. I went down to visit
Woodward and Bernstein in Washington. I'd just had an incredi-
ble couple of weeks in which I had signed up significant deals for
Bill Russell, the basketball player; Tammy Wynette, the country-

western singer; Mickey Mantle and Whitey Ford, the baseball players; and Dr. David Viscot, the psychiatrist. (I'd signed David up to do a book called *How to Live with Another Person.* At his publication party Dr. David showed up drunk and in tears . . . his wife had just left him.) Woodward and I had just finished having drinks at the Madison Hotel, across the street from the *Post.* As we headed back to the office, Bob found a dime on the sidewalk. In one swift motion he picked up the dime, put it in his pocket, pulled out a penny, and handed it to me. My ten percent agent's commission.

As you can see, money was starting to pour in. I hadn't a clue as to what I was supposed to do with it. In desperation I asked John Dean, who was now one my clients, how he'd stayed out of trouble with the IRS. (I figured if there was anyone they were going to audit it would have been John.) He told me about this wonderful institution called the business manager.

Lloyd Ziederman was John Dean's business manager. I immediately went to see him. My income had gone from three thousand dollars a year to three hundred thousand. I hadn't a clue what I was supposed to do about this kind of money, and, since I no longer lived in the commune, I didn't have that group's expert financial advice. So I loaded all of my financial records, basically a bunch of bills, receipts, and other scraps of paper, into a bag, walked into Lloyd's office, and dumped them on his desk.

"Pay my taxes and keep me out of jail," I said. Lloyd looked at the mess I called my financial life and sighed. He picked up a pad and paper and began making notes.

"Okay, how much do you want to defer into tax shelters?" I stared blankly back at him. "How much into your pension plan? You have a pension plan, don't you?"

I shook my head.

"Well, where are your assets? Are they mostly in equities, or the market, or bonds, or . . . ?" I cut him off by handing him my bankbook.

"It's all right here."

He stared at the book in horror. "All your money is in a checking account?"

I guiltily nodded my head.

Lloyd once again let out a sigh as if all the financial weight in the world was on his shoulders. This was a guy who took money seriously.

"Do you have any financial strategy for your funds?" he finally asked.

"Yeah, giving it to you."

I emptied the bag onto his desk, smiled, gave him a short salute and left.

Over the years Lloyd was able to keep me out of jail. Although I was a borderline financial idiot, he managed to always pay my bills and taxes. After the first couple of years of trying, I think he kind of gave up on teaching me the intricacies of fiscal responsibility. Each year it would be a race to see if he could get the money away from me in time to pay my taxes and bills before I spent it or gave it away.

I finally defined our relationship and got Lloyd to leave me alone by telling him the following story:

There once was a man who consistently worried about money. It would drive him nuts. He'd be miserable all the time, always worried about his financial status. One day he came home, smiling, laughing, on top of the world. His wife had never seen him like this. She asked him what had happened.

"I met a man," he said. "This man's promised to take care of all of my financial troubles."

"What do mean? How?" the wife asked.

"It's easy. For a hundred dollars a day, this guy will take care of all of my financial worries." He grinned.

"Where are you going to get a hundred dollars a day to pay him?"

"Don't you see? That's his problem now."

That's how I dealt with my finances. If anyone had a question or a problem, I'd send them to Lloyd . . . it was then his problem.

Besides being my business manager, Lloyd also became my friend. I enjoyed his company and was always welcomed in his home. One evening, I came to dinner with a bunch of Marvel Comics for his son, John. John, a precocious ten-year-old, began reading through the comics, looked up and asked, "What would happen if Spiderman and Superman had a fight?"

Lloyd and I both laughed, but John was serious. He really wanted to know. "I bet that would make a great comic," he said.

I stopped laughing. He was right.

The next day, coincidentally, I had a meeting with Stan Lee, the president of Marvel Comics. The previous year I'd approached Marvel and asked if they'd ever thought of turning their comics into books. Stan, a wonderful, cheerful, child who also happened to be in charge of the company, thought it was a great idea and let me run with it. We'd come up with a number of books that had been published and had done quite well. (Of course, if I'd been smart, I would have asked to have turned their comics into movies, but I only missed by one medium.)

Stan thought the Spiderman versus Superman idea was a winner and gave me the go-ahead to run with it. I called some friends at Warner Brothers, which owned the rights to Superman, and they too liked the idea. It was a go.

The first meeting between the creative staffs of the company was to ostensibly work out a rough story line.

Well . . . ecumenical councils in the fifth century had less rancor and debate.

"Are you nuts!" one of the illustrators screamed. "If Superman ever hit Spiderman he'd send him past Pluto!"

"Says you," the Marvel writer defiantly replied. "Spiderman would just grab onto the first building he passed and break his . . ."

"No way! He'd be broken into little pieces!"

"Way! He'd spin a kryptonite web and then kick Superman's sorry butt."

It went on like this for a full hour. Grown men, veins bulging in their necks, screaming, shrieking, howling . . . it was not a nice play date. Finally, the Spiderman team has had it. They begin packing up their stuff to leave.

I'd already promised John that this project was going to happen. I couldn't let it fall apart. I grabbed the head writer.

"What if—" I was scrambling here, "—Spiderman and Superman have this epic battle of the century . . . but they're faking it? They're really on the same team!" I could see the guy was interested. "What they're really doing is trying to lure the bad guys into action. See, if the villains think Spiderman and Superman are after each other, they'll think they're free to act and . . ."

I didn't have to go any further. They all got it. They all sat down and went to work. (The book, an oversized comic, was a huge success.)

CHARLOTTESVILLE

FEBRUARY 1975

The first thing we do, let's kill all the lawyers . . .
SHAKESPEARE, HENRY VI

John Dean was truly America's fair-haired boy. The fourth most famous Dean ever born (James, Jimmy, and Dizzy being numbers 1, 2, and 3), he had studied, worked, schemed, and clawed his way out of a boring middle-class existence to become lawyer to the president of the United States.

My mother told me when I was a boy to always be suspicious of people who had two first names, but I couldn't resist trying to contact John Dean about doing his book. I mean, the guy had actually lived out every radical's wet dream: He'd brought down Nixon.

Hays Gorey, a top-notch reporter for *Time* magazine's Washington bureau, had access to John. He'd met John during Watergate and had become a conduit to the media for him. I begged, pleaded, and implored Hays to set up a meeting for me. John had been found guilty of various crimes against the state and was going to the big house. I wanted to get to him before he went in and I wanted his book. Finally Hays relented and set up a meeting.

Dean had been the televised hero of the Watergate hearings. Cool, handsome, assured, he had methodically sliced the Nixon administration's tissue of lies into neat, easily digestible pieces of truth for the American public. Now, Dean was both adored and detested by the public. I knew his book would be a home run.

Of course, so did everyone else in the business. John was swamped with offers. Everyone from lecture agents to pornographers was trying to get to the guy. He was the flavor of the month.

I knew I'd only have one shot at him. Most likely he'd feel more comfortable with an adult agent, so I decided not to wear my McDonald's blazer or my American flag tie. I didn't fool him for a second.

At our meeting he was clearly distracted. A year ago the guy was taking the cream of America's legal profession to lunch at the White House mess, and now he was hanging out with some long-haired freak and trying to figure out what to pack for Fort Holabird Federal Prison. It was obvious he couldn't wait to get rid of me. As I rambled on about my experience in the business, John glanced at his watch. Time to drop the bomb.

"What Hays and I really wanted to talk to you about was your wife Mo doing a book."

John's body language said it all. He sat up, smiled, grabbed a notepad, and began asking questions.

It was a great idea. It would give Mo something to do while John was serving time. It would give the Deans some much-needed dough. It would allow them to tell their side of the story and it would keep her out of trouble. John loved the idea. I never mentioned his book, but I figured if I did a good job on Mo's, I'd get his as well.

I was right. *Mo*, although no artistic triumph, was a pretty good read. We got *Good Housekeeping* to take first serialization and put Mo on the cover. We got a good paperback sale. John was thrilled. Finally, he committed to me. As soon as he got out of jail, he'd let me sell his book.

In early January of 1975, John Dean was released from federal prison. His arrival at LAX, according to NBC, "rivaled Frank Sinatra's at the peak of his popularity." I arrived at the

Dean's house shortly thereafter. It was time to take control of John's life.

The first thing I did was to arrange a press conference for John. The Deans had gotten so many requests for interviews, I figured that one big one might calm the media beast. Since the press was already camped out on the doorstep, I cleverly decided to stage the interview in Dean's driveway. I also surmised that this would help us with publishers in New York. Showing John as hot copy was a way of whetting their appetites.

John had already promised an exclusive interview to Carl Stern of NBC News. Sure, I said, if the price was right. I told John that what he had to say was worth a great deal to the networks. "You gave at the office when you testified before the Watergate committee," I told him. "If they want to have you first, they'll pay."

John was incredulous. He, like most people, was sure that the network news organizations would never stoop to such measures. When I finally presented he and Mo a nice fat NBC corporate check he just shook his head—and quickly deposited it.

Things moved incredibly fast. Within a short period of time I'd managed, to quote John, "to tie up his life with a lovely green ribbon."

I had called Dick Snyder at Simon & Schuster and offered him first crack at the book. He asked me how much I wanted. "Three hundred thousand's always been a lucky number for me," I answered. He sighed and said yes.

Next I contacted Bob Walker, president of the American Program Bureau. Bob ran one of the largest lecture agencies in the world. I offered him for a speaking tour. It's not often you can actually hear drool on the phone. Bob immediately set up a full tour.

The Deans were thrilled with their newfound wealth. Everything went smoothly until a couple of days before John's first lecture, a speech at the University of Virginia. Ron Ziegler, Richard

Nixon's former press secretary and whipping boy, was also on the lecture gravy train. He'd been Nixon's chief spokesman during the coverup and now there were a lot of people who didn't think it proper for him to profit from that. Hence, students at Boston University had voted to cancel his lecture. John freaked.

Dean called and told me the lecture tour was off. He said he didn't need the anguish. The thought of facing a hostile mob scared him. He was also afraid someone might kill him. "What better place to take a shot at me than in a crowded auditorium," he pleaded. (John had received a number of death threats during the Watergate investigation, enough that the government had given him protection while he was in jail and had offered to continue it upon his release. John had turned down the offer.)

I called Bob Walker and told him John was canceling. Bob scraped himself off the ceiling and screamed, "Fine, just tell Dean he owes the University of Virginia ten grand. They've already booked the hall, sold the tickets, and bought radio and newspaper ads. He cancels, he pays."

Suddenly John was going, but with a twist. I was going with him.

On our way to Charlottesville John was a wreck. I tried to reassure him, but how do you reason with a man who's sure he's about to be shot?

We met with our university host outside the auditorium and the kid was ecstatic. They'd sold out the hall and the place was packed with television crews and newspaper reporters. I thought that was great. John looked like he wanted to throw up.

I tried again to shore up John's courage. He looked pretty shaken. Finally I turned to our host and said, "I hope you got a front row seat for me. I've got to have a good seat in case someone shoots Dean. I want to be able to get to the shooter fast and sign him up." Everyone stared at me in horror . . . except John. He cracked up. I knew he'd be okay.

John gave a terrific speech. What he'd forgotten was that he was one of the good guys. The students ate it up. He began to relax and soon he was spinning wonderful stories about what crooks he and his former partners had been. It was a masterful performance.

I spent with the next few days with John. We'd travel all day, John would give his speech, and we'd retire to some hotel or other for the night. I got to know the guy.

It was pretty weird. Here I was, a former radical, dedicated to changing the world, hanging out in a luxury hotel room with a convicted felon who just happened to be the former counsel to the president of the United States . . . and I really enjoyed the guy. Strange indeed.

John liked to come down from his speeches with a couple of drinks. I'd join him, and I'd soon be flying. One night I gave him my quick take on his former boss.

"John," I said, "imagine what kind of life Nixon would have had if his old man, Frank, hadn't got frostbite working on the streetcars in Ohio? I mean, Dick Nixon would have probably just grown up to be another boring middle-class American guy that nobody ever heard of." John stared blankly back at me.

"But instead the guy moves his family to Whittier, California, and Nixon is surrounded by Quakers." I stood up and began pacing.

"See, Whittier was a religious community, named after the poet John Greenleaf Whittier. It was a pretty intense place for little Dick to grow up in. He had to go to church meetings three times a day on Sundays. He played the organ in the Quaker meeting house. He went to Wednesday services. I'd bet that the Quakers would agree with the Catholics' old saw: 'You get a boy into the church before he's eight and you have him for life.' "

I poured myself another drink. I could tell that John was tired, so I tried to wind things up.

"I think he meant to lead a principled life, but his ambition was too great. He had too much to prove. So he started taking moral shortcuts. He paid the price of power. He sold his soul."

I finished my drink.

"I think Richard Nixon became the most guilt-ridden man ever to hold the office of president. I am convinced that there was a side of him that was so conflicted, so tortured, and so sorry that he'd disappointed his beloved mother, that he became totally self-destructive."

I could see John was trying to digest this.

"That's the key to Richard Milhous Nixon. Deep down he didn't feel he deserved any of his success. In his heart he believed that, because he'd cheated, and been dishonest, none of the glory and rewards he'd attained truly belonged to him—and worse, I believe he felt he needed to be punished. Punished by his mother's God."

I stood up and began pacing again.

"And like a true Shakespearian tragedy . . . he found a way to destroy himself. A way to bring all the mortification and humiliation he felt he deserved crashing down on his unworthy self. The dishonor of Watergate, the embarrassment of resigning the presidency, the indignity of being disbarred as a lawyer, the shame of being Richard Nixon . . . all of this was his way of dealing with the guilt he felt toward Hannah. Only by becoming the most abhorred politician in modern American politics could he assuage his poor mother's spirit."

I had never really articulated these feelings before. I looked over at John Dean, a man who had had a unique and privileged view of Nixon, for his reaction. He was fast asleep.

ROANOKE

FEBRUARY 1975

If I had to live my life again,
I'd make the same mistakes, only sooner . . .
TALLULAH BANKHEAD

I continued to travel with John Dean for the next couple of days. A limo would pick us up, take us to a private plane, and we'd fly to the site of the next speech. Every night we'd stay in another upscale hotel, have room service, and talk. It was probably how John had spent the last couple of years as White House council, but this kind of lifestyle was all new to me.

I remember one night lying in another fancy bed and thinking about what was happening to me.

I had been, like so many of my generation, sucked back into the system. WHY?

The end of the Vietnam War was one major factor. Once there was no longer a direct threat of having your tuchus blown off in Asia, many people lost interest in politics. In addition, the radical left's tactics had alienated almost everyone. They were way too violent. In the early 70s there was a major bombing a day! ROTC buildings, draft boards, federal offices. People got sick of it.

I. F. Stone's prophecy that without an agenda the kids would lose their way was correct. Hostility to government and business disappeared almost as rapidly as it came. Like a huge wave, we crashed onto the body politic, shook everything up, and then quickly receded, washed back into the giant ocean of American society.

Part of the reason we came back was the realization that the horror of the Vietnam War and the corruption of the Nixon government were personal, not institutional, failures. The basic structure of American democracy was worth preserving and fighting for. Destroying it would only result in anarchy or worse.

Meanwhile, we learned some important lessons. The Movement didn't die . . . it just shifted down a few gears and began working at a grassroots level. People whose political consciousness was raised in the 60s and 70s didn't just disappear. They began working in their communities for change. They formed cooperatives, collectives, community organizations to help take care of each other.

But the biggest change that occurred was in how we viewed each other. No longer would women, people of color, or homosexuals be easy victims for discrimination. The seeds that were planted in our Movement days continue to grow today. We helped create a system where social injustice is no longer just an obscene act, but an illegal one as well.

But the overwhelming reason that we came back, the motivation for bringing so many of us into the system, was because the rewards for participation in America were too great. It was virtually impossible to resist. Like the polio vaccine that had been given to us when we were kids, we had also been inoculated with the American Dream.

The next morning, as we were being served a lavish room service breakfast in our suite, John began to tease me about my new lifestyle. "How can you live like this?" he asked. I sat back, drank my orange juice, and smiled. I asked him if he'd ever heard of Big Bill Haywood. He hadn't.

Forty years before, Haywood had been a legendary figure in America. He was president of the Industrial Workers of the World. The IWW, or wobblies as they were called, was a group whose avowed purpose was to organize all workers in any industry into one big union. They were among the first to bring women and blacks into the labor movement. They believed the workers should tell the bosses where and when they should work, how long and for what wages, and under what kind of conditions. They were the most radical and effective organizers of the poor in American history and they scared the living daylights out of the establishment.

Anyway, after one particularly brutal confrontation with the authorities, Haywood held a press conference. Midway through it he lit up a big cigar. One of the reporters jumped to his feet and demanded to know how Mr. Haywood could reconcile the worker's struggle with his smoking an expensive one-dollar cigar.

I smiled and looked at John. "My answer to you, Mr. Dean, is the same as Big Bill's. 'Nothing's too good for the proletariat.' "

ACKNOWLEDGMENTS

After fifty-two years (my wife likes to say I'm forty-twelve) of living I've found that it's a good idea upon meeting old acquaintances to simply apologize. This saves both time and explanation and seems to make everyone feel better. So, before I get into a detailed list of acknowledgments, I'd like to apologize to everyone mentioned in this book, everyone who helped put this book together, and just to be on the safe side, everyone I've ever known.

A number of people were instrumental in making *Too Good To Be Forgotten*. First and foremost I have to thank my editor and pal Myles Thompson. Myles, with his unflagging enthusiasm, generous counsel, and extraordinary intelligence, made this book happen. His able sidekick, Jennifer Pincott, climbed into the trenches with me and was a constant source of inspiration and common sense. Her editing was patient yet firm, and her positive energy helped shape the book into something that I'm proud of.

Ann McCarthy and Peter Knapp were both extraordinarily helpful with their keen insight and marketing and editorial suggestions. Lori Sayde-Mehrtens and Ellen Silberman gave me invaluable advice on how to deal with the media in a clear and focused manner. Janice Weisner spearheaded the production process, Stephanie Landis of North Market Street Graphics made

my work read like it was written by a grown-up, and Beth Ober-
holtzer made it look elegant. Thanks to Liz Hock for her helpful
suggestions. George Stanley and Dean Karrel have done a fantastic job of getting the books into stores, and Renea Perry has been
a champ in helping keep track of all the pieces of the puzzle.
Finally, Lee Thompson was a terrific cheerleader and friend. To
all the wonderful people of John Wiley & Sons, thank you.

I'd like to thank a number of friends who patiently sat on the
phone as I breathlessly read excerpts to them. To Charlie Firestone, John Rothchild, Susan Wolfe, Margarie Walker, Larry Stein-
man, Anne Taylor Fleming, Susie Toigo, Nancy Craig, Lynn and
Frank Kirk, Bo Burlingham, and Carol Corcoran . . . thank you.

I'd also like to thank a couple of friends who read the manuscript and gave me valuable advice. Seymour Hersh, Derek
Shearer, Taylor Branch, and Kitty Kelley were fantastically generous with their time and wisdom.

Bonnie Goldstein and Jim Grady have been there for me in both
my life and this book; a special thank you to both of them, and to
their daughter Rachel, who helped research parts of the book.

My son Oliver Obst was a fantastic sounding board for this
work. Oly's open, honest appraisal of the book was invaluable and
his enthusiastic response spurred me on.

Finally, to my precious wife Jane, the prime mover, my deepest
thanks. If this book works at all it's because of the love, acceptance, and confidence that Jane has poured into me. This book is
for her.

INDEX